Humanism in Language Teaching

A critical perspective

Earl W. Stevick

Oxford University Press 1990

Oxford University Press
Walton Street, Oxford OX2 6DP

Oxford New York Toronto
Delhi Bombay Calcutta Madras Karachi
Petaling Jaya Singapore Hong Kong Tokyo
Nairobi Dar es Salaam Cape Town
Melbourne Auckland

and associated companies in
Berlin Ibadan

Oxford, and *Oxford English* are trade marks of Oxford University Press

ISBN 0 19 437161 1

© Oxford University Press 1990

Printed in Great Britain by Thomson Litho, East Kilbride, Scotland.

Acknowledgements

The publishers would like to thank the following for their permission to use copyright material:

Academic Press Ltd., a subsidiary of Harcourt Brace Jovanovich, and E. Perecman, for extracts from 'Spontaneous translation and language mixing in a polyglot aphasic' by E. Perecman published in *Brain and Language* 1984, Vol. 23; Cambridge University Press for extracts from *Communicating Naturally in a Second Language* by Wilga M. Rivers, CUP 1983, and *Images and Options in the Language Classroom* by E.W. Stevick, CUP 1986; Educational Solutions Inc., for extracts from *The Adolescent and His Self* (c) 1962 by C. Gattegno, *In the Beginning There Were No Words: The Universe of Babies* (c) 1976 by C. Gattegno, *The Common Sense of Teaching Foreign Languages* (c) 1976 by C. Gattegno, and *On Being Freer* (c) 1988 by C. Gattegno; Faber and Faber Ltd., and Random House Inc., for an extract from 'Horae Canonicae: vespers' from *Selected Poems of W.H. Auden* (c) 1955 W.H. Auden; Houghton Mifflin & Co. for an extract from *Becoming a Person* by Carl Rogers (c) 1961 by Houghton Mifflin & Co.; Newbury House Publishers, a division of Harper & Row Publishers Inc., for a short extract from *Methods that Work* by J. Oller and P. Richard-Amato (c) 1983 by Newbury House Publishers, and an extract from *Memory, Meaning and Method* by E.W. Stevick (c) 1976 by Newbury House Publishers; Prentice-Hall Publishers for an extract from *Principles of Language Learning and Language Teaching* by H.D. Brown (c) by Prentice-Hall; R.C. Roberts for extracts from his article 'Therapy for the Saints' published in *Christianity Today*, Vol. 29, no. 16, 1985; Sheed and Ward Inc., for extracts from *Counseling and Psychotherapy: the Pursuit of Values* by Charles A. Curran (c) 1968 by Sheed and Ward Inc.; Sir Karl Popper for extracts from his book *Unended Quest*, 1974 Glasgow: Collins.

At the author's request, the royalties from this book are being divided between TESOL and IATEFL.

Contents

Author and series editor   1
Foreword   3
Preface   4

1 Karl Popper and the power of words   7

1.1 Why start with Popper?   7
1.2 Popper's scientific approach   8
1.3 Comments on Popper's approach   13
1.4 Language teaching in Popper's worlds   19

2 Humanism   21

2.1 A semantic thicket   21
2.2 'Humanism' outside language education   21
2.3 'Humanism' in the writings of language teachers   24
2.4 A tentative map of the humanisms   28
2.5 The 'stance of despair', and three remedies for it   31

3 Using words: metaphor   35

3.1 Metaphor: what it is and how it works   35
3.2 Three general metaphors in the study of language   39
3.3 Four 'humanistic' metaphors   45
3.4 Summary   54

4 Other aspects of the discussion of 'humanism'   55

4.1 Matters of form   55
4.2 Matters of substance   62
4.3 Summary   68

5 The 'humanism' of Charles A. Curran   71

5.1   A glimpse of Curran's approach in action   71
5.2   Two elusive concepts: 'incarnation' and 'redemption'   77
5.3   'Incarnation' and 'redemption': a traditional view   86
5.4   Counseling-Learning: theory and practice   95
5.5   Counseling-Learning and the humanisms   98

6 A second 'humanistic' educator: Caleb Gattegno   101

6.1   Introduction   101
6.2   Basic concepts   107
6.3   The self and its creatures   111
6.4   Knowing and learning   115
6.5   How should we live?   119
6.6   Commentary   124

7 Humanistic elements outside the 'humanistic' methods   131

7.1   Humanism in two of the 'humanisms'   131
7.2   Humanistic elements in other approaches   132
7.3   'Empiricism' and 'rationalism' in language teaching   137
7.4   Summary of this book   143

Bibliography   145

Index   153

Author and series editor

Earl Stevick has been a learner, teacher, and teacher trainer since 1938. Since his retirement in 1984 from the Foreign Service Institute, he has taught a course on language learning at the University of Maryland, Baltimore County. He also occasionally does voluntary teaching of ESL. His first book for language teachers appeared in 1957: his more recent publications include *Memory, Meaning and Method* (1976), *Teaching Languages: A Way and Ways* (1980), and *Images and Options in the Language Classroom* (1986).

Alan Maley worked for The British Council from 1962-1988, serving as English Language Officer in Yugoslavia, Ghana, Italy, France, and China, and as Regional Representative for The British Council in South India (Madras). He is currently Director-General of the Bell Educational Trust, Cambridge.

He wrote *Quartet* (with Françoise Grellet and Wim Welsing, OUP 1982). He has also written *Beyond Words, Sounds Interesting, Sounds Intriguing, Words, Variations on a Theme,* and *Drama Techniques in Language Learning* (all with Alan Duff), *The Mind's Eye* (with Françoise Grellet and Alan Duff), and *Learning to Listen* and *Poem into Poem* (with Sandra Moulding). He is also series editor for the Resource Books for Teachers and the Oxford Supplementary Skills.

Foreword

Earl Stevick's book is the first of a new series intended to stimulate and provoke thought, reflection, and debate. As such, it seems wholly appropriate to these aims.

The book is about the need for clarity - of language and of thought; about meaning what we say and about seeking to understand properly what others are attempting to say. It is itself eminently humanistic in its striving after an understanding of others, while remaining rigorously intellectual in its pursuit of objectivity. This reflects the author's belief that we need both rational and non-rational bases for action, and that we function best when 'faith', experience, and intellect are in harmony.

A major objective of the book is to undertake a critical examination of 'humanism', both in its general sense and with specific reference to language teaching: what the word itself has meant or could mean, the ways in which some commentators have used language to criticize it, and the language in which its proponents have set forth their views. Stevick shares with Karl Popper the belief that such things need to be made explicit before rational discussion is possible. His careful yet ruthless dissection of the flabby under-belly of language will enrage some and delight others. And his detailed critical analysis of the terminology of both Curran and Gattegno will be of great value to all those who, till now, have only experienced these thinkers at second- or third-hand.

He has made a characteristically honest attempt to make his own writing consistent with the views on clarity he is expressing by purging it of anything which might colour or distort the judgment of his readers. To use his own description of Popper's writing: 'His prose ... is as clean as his content is honest.' Yet, behind this reserve, there is a passionate concern which perhaps represents humanism - in every sense of the word - at its best.

Alan Maley

4

Preface

'A nice technique, but is it culturally sensitive?' asked one of Mark Clarke's graduate students after watching a teaching demonstration one day. Clarke (1982) points out that this sort of question, no matter what is being queried, often carries an air of implied judgment. To borrow Clarke's metaphor, such questions give the impression of looking down on the ignorant toiling masses of one's colleagues from the top of one bandwagon or another. Another difficulty with questions of this kind is that their meanings are almost never well-defined. We may each of us have a very clear feeling of what it means to be 'culturally sensitive' or 'cost-effective' or 'humanistic'. We may even have a very clear feeling that that very clear feeling of ours is shared by all our colleagues - or at least by all those who are intellectually both alert and honest. Frequently, however, we have not formulated those feelings explicitly even to ourselves, and we might be hard put to do so. But unwritten and ambiguous standards lead too easily to confusion, and sometimes to unnecessary dispute.

This book therefore has four aims. The first is simply to examine how we language teachers have used words and word-pictures in talking about one recent set of approaches and techniques - those labeled 'humanistic'. The words and sentences that have been used in our discussions have come from two kinds of sources. Some sources are rational; that is, they are based on disciplined observation, on experimental work in cognitive science, and on reason. Other sources are non-rational; they are based on intuition, and on assumptions that have not been tested either because they are untestable, or because we haven't got round to testing them, or because we are unwilling to test them. Alan Maley (1983) has pointed out that for some or all proponents of 'humanistic' approaches (and, he might have added, for some or all opponents of those same approaches) such untested assumptions are hidden but very powerful. They are, he says, comparable to the assumptions that lead to acceptance or rejection of what are called religions. Our second aim will therefore be to look at these untested assumptions - at what we shall call the 'faiths' - that may motivate advocates of the 'humanistic' approaches and their critics. Our third aim will be to attempt to remedy a certain lack of information that appears to exist, particularly with regard to the theory and practice of two frequently cited approaches to 'humanistic' language teaching: Curran's Counseling-Learning and Gattegno's Science of Education. Finally, we shall look briefly at humanism (without inverted commas) in methods that are not commonly labeled 'humanistic' from grammar-translation on down to the present day. If we succeed in these four aims, we may hope to have contributed toward tidying up an area of innovation and controversy in which this writer has been involved during about half his career.

This is first of all a book about 'humanism' - and humanism - in the teaching of languages. By implication, however, it also addresses a broader issue: the difficulty, even in scientific and scholarly discussions, of maintaining discourse that is strictly scholarly and scientific. Comparable difficulty was evident three decades ago in exchanges between representatives of structuralist and transformational generative linguistics. Still earlier, the same was true for advocates of the behaviorist-influenced pedagogies, and theorists who adhered to a more traditional approach to teaching. Needless to say, this difficulty has also been evident through the centuries in scholarly discussions completely unrelated to either the description or the teaching of languages. No doubt it will arise from time to time in the future, both inside and outside our profession, in relation to topics we cannot now predict.

Christopher Brumfit, Caleb Gattegno, Peter O'Connell, and Jennybelle Rardin have been notable for their patience as well as for their constructive suggestions during the writing of this book. I am grateful to them and to the following colleagues for helpful comments on various parts of earlier drafts: Bill Acton, Marianne Celce-Murcia, Mark Clarke, Clifton de Córdoba, Karl Diller, Madeline Ehrman, Olaf Heck, Stephen D. Krashen, Diane Larsen-Freeman, Donald N. Larson, Jack Millet, John Oller, Adrian Palmer, Tom Scovel, William A. Smalley, Claire Stanley, Daniel Tranel, the entire faculty of the Master of Arts in Teaching Languages Program of the School for International Training, and my students in the 1989 TESOL Summer Institute of San Francisco State University. I would also like to thank Michelle Persons, Robert C. Roberts, and Jess Stribling for bibliographical references. Shakti Gattegno cheerfully tracked down certain quotations in Chapter 6. Anne Conybeare's editorial guidance was meticulous and invariably helpful. As always, my wife Betty Rae has given indispensable intellectual and moral support throughout the project.

Earl Stevick
Arlington, Virginia

1 Karl Popper and the power of words

1.1 Why start with Popper?

During the 1970s, the language teaching profession was introduced to a number of unconventional methodologies, the most visible of which were Total Physical Response, the Silent Way, Community Language Learning, and Suggestopedia. For many of us involved with 'humanistic' language teaching, that was a time of great enthusiasm. A number of years have passed, and one still hears papers on those methodologies, and one talks with teachers who are making effective use of them. But the initial excitement has been replaced by the familiarity of daily practice. It is now time for enthusiasm to be matched by careful thought.

In *Teaching Languages: A Way and Ways* (Stevick 1980), I outlined the principles of three 'humanistic' methodologies and gave examples of how they worked in the classroom. That book warned that it represented the author's viewpoint only, and that the new approaches might not be for everyone. Nevertheless, its purpose was to encourage others to study them seriously. The book did not, however, anticipate the degree to which those new approaches, perhaps even more than earlier methodological innovations, often either challenged or confirmed unexamined assumptions at a very deep level.

In an important critique of 'humanism' in language teaching, Alan Maley (1983) described that deep level of response as 'religious' or 'quasi-religious'. He believed that some teachers were blindly accepting this or that body of dogma, which was just clear enough to be convincing but vague enough to be unassailable. Having done so, they were rejecting all they had thought or done before, and looking askance at colleagues still mired in what they regarded as the errors of the past. Instead of keeping their eyes open, Maley charged, and instead of continuing to think for themselves, these newly-converted teachers were resigning those duties to gurus. In two other important papers (1982a, 1982b), Christopher Brumfit voiced the same misgivings. Both writers called for critical examination of the 'humanistic' approaches, and both recommended the philosopher Karl Popper as a model for the kind of thinking needed.

This book is intended as just such an examination of 'humanistic' language teaching. The present chapter will summarize Popper's critical stance as he presented it in his intellectual autobiography *Unended Quest* (1976). In the rest of the book, we shall attempt to remain consistent with that stance in answering six questions:

- ☐ What can we mean by 'humanism'? (Chapter 2)
- ☐ How has imprecise use of words interfered with clear thinking both within and about the 'humanistic' methodologies? (Chapters 3 and 4)
- ☐ What are the main tenets behind Curran's Community Language Learning? (Chapter 5)
- ☐ What are the main tenets behind Gattegno's Silent Way? (Chapter 6)
- ☐ How do humanistic principles show up in certain approaches not ordinarily called 'humanistic'? (Chapter 7)
- ☐ What unchallenged assumptions (what 'faiths') may be tied to the acceptance - or rejection - of the positions discussed in this book?

1.2 Popper's scientific approach

1.2.1 Three worlds

In *Unended Quest*, Karl Popper speaks of three 'worlds'. What he calls world 1 is the world of 'things' - of tables and chairs, actual photographs and paintings, and the like (p.181). World 2 contains subjective experiences, for example the perceptions formed out of the audible, visible, and tangible events in our classrooms. The world-2 object - one person's subjective experience or impression - may be *different from* another person's world-2 object, but it cannot *contradict* it (ibid.). World 3 - the world with which Popper is most concerned - is 'the world of statements in themselves' (ibid.), including problems, theories, and critical arguments. Again relating Popper's ideas to the field of language teaching, world 3 presumably includes our generalizations from experience, all the way from one-sentence maxims to full-blown methods. The objects in world 3 are created by human beings.

It is clear that when he speaks of 'statements in themselves', Popper is referring not so much to wording as to content. He says that the relationship between a theory (or other statement) and the words in which it is cast is comparable to the relationship that exists between written words and the letters that have been used in writing them down. Both these relationships are relatively superficial and transient. Nevertheless it is expedient, if not absolutely necessary, for us to put theories into words:

> The decisive thing seems to me that we can put objective thoughts - that is, theories - before us in such a way that we can criticize them and argue about them. To do so, we must formulate them in some more or less permanent (especially linguistic) form. (p.182)

In world 3, unlike world 2, the content of one person's thought may contradict the content of another person's thought. For that matter, different parts of the same person's thought may be mutually contradictory. And contradiction is the raw material for argument. Therefore, 'the argumentative function of language became particularly important for me because I regarded it as the basis of all critical thought' (p.74). Objects from world 2 may provide the subject matter for objects in world 3:

> I do not deny the existence of subjective experiences, of mental states, of intelligences, and of minds; I even believe these to be of the utmost importance. But I think that our theories about these subjective experiences, or about these minds, should be as objective as other theories. And by an objective theory I mean a theory which is arguable, which can be exposed to rational criticism, preferably a theory which can be tested: one which does not merely appeal to our subjective intuitions. (p.138)

1.2.2 Scientific method

Popper discusses both the aim and the method of science. With regard to the former, 'According to my view, finding theories which are better approximations to truth is what the scientist aims at; the aim of science is knowing more and more' (p.150). Later in the book he says that *objective truth and its growth* remains throughout the intellectual world the highest value of all (p.195).

Scientific method consists of two steps. First it is necessary, working in world 3 ('the world of statements in themselves'), to arrive at and to state some expectation about future events. Popper at various times calls such an expectation a dogma, a myth, a hypothesis, a theory, or (one of his favorite words) a conjecture. He writes 'Critical thinking must have before it something to criticize, and this, I thought, must be the result of dogmatic thinking' (p.41). The second step, which differentiates Popper's view of science from the ideas of some whom he criticizes, is to test each statement immediately, with an eye not to the confirmation of the statement, but to its disconfirmation:

> The critical method [is] the method of trial and error: the method of proposing bold hypotheses, and exposing them to the severest criticism, in order to detect where we have erred. (p.86)

> I arrived at the conclusion that the scientific attitude was the critical attitude, which did not look for verifications but for crucial tests; tests which could *refute* the theory tested, though they could never establish it. (p.38) [emphasis in original]

If we seek only confirmation, after all, we are placing ourselves in constant danger of fallacious reasoning. For example, in one of the classical syllogistic forms of Aristotelian logic:

If A, then B.	If the cat ate the fish, the fish is gone.
B is true.	The fish is gone.
Therefore A is true.	Therefore the cat must have eaten it.

The search for disconfirmation appears to be what writers who cite Popper have in mind when they refer to 'falsifiability'. (The quotation from page 38 of Popper's autobiography given above implies that 'verification', which is sometimes regarded as a criterion for scientific respectability, has no standing in Popper's system.) Popper holds that this disconfirmation must be sought consciously and actively: 'Only tests undertaken in a *critical* spirit - attempted refutations - should count [toward corroboration of a theory]' (p.103).

When Popper talks about the scientific goal of 'knowing more and more', he seems to mean something like 'building an ever more comprehensive body of not-yet-disconfirmed conjectures'. In his own words: 'Traditional philosophy linked the ideal of rationality with final, demonstrable knowledge ... while I linked it with the *growth of conjectural knowledge*' (p.149).

Although problems and hypotheses and arguments are world-3 creations of the human mind, their fate is not entirely within human control:

> ... critical discussion assesses the submitted theories in terms of their rational or intellectual value as solutions to the problem under consideration; and as regards their truth, or nearness to truth. *Truth is the main regulative principle* in the criticism of theories; their power to raise new problems and to solve them is another. (p.22) [emphasis added]

For Popper, theories and arguments are human artifacts; truth, apparently, is not. But just as truth stands outside human control, so it is also beyond human grasp, and for this reason we are never rationally justified in believing in anything in world 3:

> When we think we have found an approximation to the truth in the form of a scientific theory which has stood up to criticism and to tests better than its competitors, we shall, as realists, accept it as a basis for practical action, simply because we have nothing better (or nearer the truth). But we need not accept it as true: we need not believe in it ... (p.151)

'Final truth', then, is not what we are trying to find: 'The only *intellectually* important ends are: the formulation of problems; the tentative proposing of theories to solve them; and the critical discussion of the competing theories' (p.22) [emphasis added].

To summarize Popper's 'critical method':

- ☐ Using any means - intuition, insight, or painstaking investigation of phenomena - arrive at some conjecture about what will or will not happen under a given set of circumstances.
- ☐ Put this conjecture into language. '*If* such-and-such conditions exist, *then* this thing is likely to happen, and that thing is not likely to happen.'
- ☐ Scrutinize (the ideas behind) the language, testing for circularities or internal inconsistencies.
- ☐ Test the predictions for consistency with the external world.
- ☐ Discard any conjecture that has failed any test. Tentatively retain any conjecture that has not yet failed a test.

1.2.3 Scientific attitude

Popper expresses admiration for the non-dogmatic attitude of Einstein, who himself listed certain tests that would make his Theory of Relativity untenable. But while it may be handy, neat, and otherwise pleasant to be offered a theory that comes with its own prepackaged set of potential refutations, Popper says that this is not necessary. What is desirable is testability, i.e. a conjecture must possess the qualities that enable it to pass - or to fail - a certain test. The system thus depends on the user's ability both to define and to measure all of the terms within a given conjecture. For example, the conjecture ' "Pluviosity" is what causes rain' is circular. But the conjecture 'The probability of rain can be predicted on the basis of changes in the density of the air' is not circular, and is equivalent to a whole series of statements such as:

> If W (a particular pattern of air density), then Y (a particular probability of rain).

> If X (some other pattern of air density), then not Z (some other probability of rain).

In the second conjecture, all of the terms are clearly defined and Y and Z are measurable. Without a barometer, however, W and X would not be measurable, and so the testability - the scientific standing - of the conjecture depends on the availability of a certain technology.

It appears, then, that Popper's 'critical method' is well suited for learning about quarks or continental drift or the causes of cancer. Conjectures about these subjects may be quite subtle, and the measurements required for testing them may be incredibly sensitive, utilizing highly sophisticated technology. Nevertheless, any one of these measurements in itself is essentially simple. Popper himself points out that there are limitations to his method, that critical tests are characteristic of science, but that there are many areas for which testability is not available. Ideas may be 'criticizable though not testable' (p.151); a philosophical thesis may be 'clearly wrong even though irrefutable' (p.187), and a conjecture may 'have some explanatory power even though ... it is difficult to test' (p.189). Even here, though, he feels that:

> The critical *method*, though it will use tests wherever possible, and preferably practical tests, can be generalized into ... the critical or rational *attitude*, [the essence of which is] readiness to be criticized and eagerness to criticize oneself, [and that this] critical attitude of reasonableness should be extended as far as possible. (p.115) [emphasis added]

For Popper, the search for disconfirmation is thus only one result of an underlying attitude. This quest is to be pursued wherever the subject matter permits, but it is not essential to what Popper would consider rational discourse.

Indeed, he extends world 3 beyond 'problems, theories, and critical arguments' which he regards as 'a world 3 in the narrow sense' (p.187). He gives examples of the 'broader world 3':

[A] state of intense mental activity which is not self-conscious is reached ... in intellectual or artistic work: in trying to understand a problem, or a theory; or in enjoying an absorbing work of fiction, or perhaps in playing the piano or playing a game of chess. In such states, we may forget where we are. ... What our mind is engaged in, with the utmost concentration, is the attempt to grasp a world 3 object, or to produce it. (p.191)

World 3 in the wider sense comprises not only the products of our intellect ... but also the products of our mind in a much wider sense; for example, the products of our imagination. ... Myths and fictions should not be excluded from world 3. So we are led to include art and, in fact, all human products into which we have injected some of our ideas, and which incorporate the result of *criticism* (in a sense wider than merely intellectual criticism). (p.195) [emphasis in original]

1.3 Comments on Popper's approach

1.3.1 Limitations of Popper's position

Popper's writing is both stimulating and convincing, and his willingness to extend his principles to matters of the arts and imagination is interesting. Basically, however, he does seem to work within an acknowledged boundary. Near the beginning of his book he says, '*In matters of the intellect*, the only things worth striving for are true theories ...' (p.22) [emphasis added], and again near the end, '*Throughout this human intellectual world 3*, ... objective truth and its growth remains the highest value of all' (p.195) [emphasis added]. But - to paraphrase a statement in Alan Maley's 1983 paper - although there are analogies to be drawn between the nature and complexity of life and the nature and complexity of the intellectual search for truer theories, they are not the same. Searching for truer theories is only one part of the life experience. Popper advises 'realists' to find out which scientific theory 'has stood up to criticism and to tests better than its competitors, [and then to] accept it as *a* basis for practical action' (p.151) [emphasis added]. He also tells us what he means by 'rational' action:

We may first replace the idea of belief by that of action; and we may say that actions (or inactions) are 'rational' if they are carried out in accordance with the state, prevailing at the time, of the critical scientific discussion. There is no better synonym for 'rational' than 'critical.' (Belief ... is never rational: it is rational to *suspend* belief.) (p.87) [emphasis in original]

We may agree with Popper that if one does not avail oneself of the most-successful-to-date theory, one is not being realistic or rational. But we must also recognize that practical action is often based on more than knowledge of intellectual theories and their rational evaluation. Any action that is of any consequence is derived from a mixture of sources, some - but only some - of which are intellectual. Insofar as 'living' means acting, 'the life experience', in Maley's phrase, consists in finding, choosing, and following up on *a full range* of bases for actions, *including the action of assenting to an intellectual position*. Some of these bases are rational, but some are not. If this is true for 'the life experience' as a whole, then we should not be surprised to find it true also for various parts of the life experience as well, including the making of furniture (which Popper decided not to do), or the making and testing of conjectures (which he did do), or even the learning and teaching of foreign languages.

My concern is that appreciation of the potential beauty of 'world-3 objects', coupled with an awareness of their power and of the need for handling them with the greatest care, may lead (wrongly) to the belief that they are sufficient for dealing with all important problems. This is the belief portrayed by Thomas More, who, in his well-known book *Utopia* (1516), described an ideal society. The fundamental achievement of the Utopians was that they had succeeded in crafting and maintaining a small set of just the right 'very few laws', which were of course 'world-3 objects'. Even if More was writing partly with tongue in cheek, he here captures a perennial tendency in human striving. We will meet a Utopian again in 2.4.

1.3.2 Emotion and Popper's position

Bases for action fall into at least two categories. One, as Popper has shown, is intellectual or rational. The other is non-intellectual, and includes the emotions. Of course, neither ever works entirely alone. One tradition holds with Alexander Pope, who wrote in his *Essay on Man* (1734), that

> ... all subsists by elemental strife;
> and passions are the elements of life,

and that

> The surest virtues thus from passions shoot,
> Wild nature's vigor working at the root.

That is to say, the initiative for action originates in the non-rational side of human nature. This position contrasts with Popper's. For him, emotions are 'subjective experiences', and therefore fall within his world 2. In some ways his treatment of emotions is the least convincing part of his whole book. In his discussion of music, Popper is adamant that the composer's emotions are not the source of his or her music; rather, the composer reacts emotionally (and in other ways as well) to what he or she has written, and the emotions thus become one of several bases for criticizing and revising the music:

> According to my objectivist theory (which does not deny self-expression but stresses its utter triviality) the really interesting function of the composer's emotions is not that they are to be expressed, but that they may be used to test the success or the fittingness of the (objective) work. (p.67)

But if we try to extend this reasoning to the everyday use of language, we are forced to say that the role of emotion in shaping the words of a declaration of love, or of a temper tantrum, is also 'utterly trivial'. Such a position is hard to accept.

Similarly, Popper minimizes the power of music to arouse emotions in people other than the composer: '[The theory] that music has the power to arouse emotions and to soothe them, ... to make [man] brave [or] turn him into a coward ... exaggerates the power of music, to say the least' (p.66). We may ask what Popper would make of the experimentally demonstrated and commercially exploited power of music to enhance emotional reactions to movies or television commercials, or to get people into fast food restaurants but keep them from staying too long. Similarly, in language we have rhetoric. As I understand the term, rhetoric is the use of language in order to influence action by whatever means seem likely to be effective, to persuade rather than to reason. It would appear that these examples of the ways in which music and rhetoric are used illustrate the importance of the non-rational as a partial basis for action, including the hearer's or reader's action of accepting an argument.

But if this is indeed the case, what is the role - what are the responsibilities - of a person who is skilled in shaping the emotional reactions of other people either overtly or otherwise? This question becomes all the more urgent if emotions are indeed important factors in forming bases for action, and if we consider the adoption of a way of thinking to be one kind of action. Popper quotes a position described by Plato, that '[the use of] any rhetorical knowledge or skill would be dishonest trickery and deception' (p.66), presumably if it is used to influence the behavior of readers or hearers. Although Popper himself apparently rejects this position, his own book is consistent with it, for his writing is notably free of rhetorical devices that might lead readers to agree with him for non-intellectual reasons. Popper writes, as he says, 'with [an imaginary reader] constantly looking over my shoulder and ... pointing out to me passages which are not clear (p.83). His prose in his autobiography is consequently as clean as his content is honest.

1.3.3 Values and Popper's position

A second category of non-intellectual bases for action includes beliefs about how things fit together in life, about what is desirable, and about what gives meaning to existence - the kinds of things that Popper, in a reference to Beethoven, called his 'hopes, his secret dreams, and his heroic fight against despair' (p.61). To some extent, certainly

> one way of life [one overall disposition toward one set of actions and not another? EWS] may be incompatible with another way of life in *almost* the same sense in which a theory may be logically incompatible with another. These incompatibilities are there, objectively, even if we are unaware of them. And so our purposes and our aims, like our theories, may compete, and may be critically compared and discussed. (p.195) [emphasis added]

Popper does not elaborate on why he used the word 'almost' here, but again he would have fitted into the court of good King Utopus, the founder of Utopia, who foresaw that in discussions of religion, 'the truth of its own power would at the last issue out and come to light *so [long as] the matter were handled with reason'* . (p.240) [emphasis added]

On a very large scale, however, it is difficult to see how it would be possible to make rational comparisons between ways of life as world-3 objects. Popper says that the *value* of theories, beliefs, and other inventions consists in their 'being of help in solving a problem' (p.194). But *the choice and ranking of problems to be solved* ultimately lies beyond rational evaluation. Popper's own approach provides an example of the underlying influence of the non-rational, for regardless of its intellectual merits, it is a position that should be comfortable for anyone who, like Popper, would prefer to see every 'problem soluble from a rational point of view' (p.186). Similarly, the belief that nothing is worth believing should have a non-rational appeal to anyone who, for whatever reason, has a deep reluctance to make a commitment to religious or other large-scale beliefs that are beyond logical proof (see Brumfit 1982a, p.18). Even if my speculations about certain non-rational side benefits of Popper's approach are correct, it is, of course, still possible that some people who adopt it may have no interest at all in those benefits. Nevertheless, the all-encompassing status of the non-rational is movingly illustrated in the final paragraph of Popper's autobiographical work:

> If I am right in my conjecture that we grow, and become ourselves, only in interaction with world 3, then the fact that we can all contribute to this world, if only a little, can give comfort to everyone; and especially to one who *feels* that in struggling with ideas *he has found more happiness* than he could ever *deserve*. (p.196) [emphasis added]

Popper's closing statement contrasts with a paragraph found near the end of another autobiographical book, this one by Oliver Sacks (1984), the author of *Awakenings* and *The Man Who Mistook His Wife for a Hat*:

> When I first became a doctor and decided to enter neurology, there was a part of me that wanted only the pure joy and challenge of concepts - abstractions divorced from any human reality. This, I think, is not uncommon among neurologists. ... In 'pure' medicine, the questions of existence, deep and terrible, were neatly excluded. This was 'safe' - but it was also a sort of death, a cutting-off from the rich phenomenality of experience, the phenomena of sickness and health alike. (p.202)

1.3.4 Faith

My position, then, is that:

- ☐ The 'total life experience' (which includes cabinet-making, philosophizing, language teaching, and many other activities) includes everything we do - our actions and reactions.
- ☐ How we act and react is based not only on critical judgment of competing intellectual conjectures, but also on needs, and on perceptions that have accumulated out of individual experience.
- ☐ Some of the needs that underlie action are non-rational, and some of the perceptions are erroneous or irrelevant, and therefore misleading.

In this book, we shall use the word 'faith' to stand for whatever bases for action we have not subjected to Popperian critical judgment, either because they are simply not the kinds of things that *can* be judged critically, or because we have attempted critical judgment and remained unconvinced of its results, or because we have not got round to examining them in that way, or because we are unwilling to do so. Articles of faith are sometimes subtle, pervasive, unrecognized, and therefore very powerful. They also frequently have a certain amount of emotion attached to them. For example, this writer once remarked to a fellow graduate student that he supposed everyone had strong beliefs of one kind or another, whether of a conventionally religious or other nature. The other student's response, as he banged his fist into his palm, was, 'Well, *I* have no strong beliefs!'

Then what is the relationship between the Popperian 'critical attitude' and this kind of 'faith'? Within certain well-defined exercises in the world of the intellect, it may be possible to do without 'faith' entirely, or almost entirely. In the world at large, however, there is need for both. If in a practical undertaking such as language teaching we try to act or react only on the basis of what has passed all Popperian tests, we will be severely limited. If, on the other hand, we act entirely from instinct - from unconsidered, intuitive 'faith' based only on our own private store of experience - we are very likely to get ourselves and our students into trouble. Surely neither extreme position is necessary, and neither is wise.

Perhaps the best course is not to minimize or deny 'faith' in the sense in which we are using that word. It is rather to develop and enrich faith through our own experiences and whatever we can learn of the experiences of others, and then to test that faith constantly against reason and subsequent experience. In this process, critical judgment may lead to a higher round of faith. Faith will alternately be enlarged and reduced and enlarged again and reduced again, and will become less and less likely to mislead, more likely to steer us right. Faith may also find instruction in whatever variety of 'holy writ' it can commit itself to, whether that writ comes from Carl Rogers or from Karl Popper or from more traditional sources. Perhaps a good rule of thumb would be 'Hold as little faith as possible, but as much as necessary.' In practice this is probably not far from what Maley (1983) and Brumfit (1982a, 1982b) have recommended, though they state it somewhat differently.

In Chapters 5 to 7, we shall examine the faiths that appear to lie behind the work of a number of people who are active in education. Popper's faith, by his own description, includes 'the existence of regularities in our world' (p.150), but it appears also to include the belief that he has found no less 'happiness' in the world for his having 'struggled with ideas' rather than becoming a cabinet-maker or a contemplative monk, and further that the world would be better off if people would use critical judgment in all they do, rather than acting on the basis of unexamined experience. Whether he was right, or only partly right, or wrong, is not the question here. The point here is that these beliefs are further examples of conjectures - conjectures that are not themselves subject to testing or to potential falsifiability. They are faith.

1.4   Language teaching in Popper's worlds

1.4.1 Approaches, methods, techniques, and movements

In Anthony's classic definition, an 'approach' to language teaching is 'a set
of correlative assumptions', and Richards and Rodgers (1986, p.16) follow
Anthony in their use of this word. It is therefore clear that what we call an
'approach' is a member of Popper's world 3. Similarly, descriptions of
whole methods and even of techniques, are world-3 objects. What we
observe when we visit classes are acts - world-1 objects that are derived from
those world-3 objects and are more or less consistent with them. An even
broader term than 'approach' is 'movement', which is generally used to
stand for world-1 activities that sometimes - though seldom - receive explicit
world-3 descriptions.

We language teachers commonly try to shape our own and one another's
behavior by means of world-3 objects such as these. The question is whether
they are parts of 'world 3 in a narrow sense', where their falsification is
feasible; or whether, along with the other products of our imagination -
products which cannot be subjected to 'critical tests' but which may still be
handled with 'the critical or rational attitude [of] readiness to be criticized
and eagerness to criticize oneself' (p.115) - they are parts of world 3 only in
the wider sense described in 1.2.3.

1.4.2 Two maxims

One formulation which has considerable appeal for teachers, and which we
would therefore hope to find attackable, arguable, defensible, even testable,
is a maxim of Brumfit's:

> Only when there are messages being carried which are significant to
> users will there be full engagement with the linguistic code. (1984,
> p.122)

Or, in the style of my summary of Popper's 'critical method':

> *If* the messages being carried are not significant to users,
> *then* there will be less than full engagement with the linguistic code.

This statement is probably an example of what Popper, in his non-pejorative
sense of the word, would call 'dogma'. Some questions immediately present
themselves. When is a message 'significant', for example, and when is it
not? What can we mean by 'engagement' with the linguistic code, and when
is engagement 'full'? Perhaps what Brumfit meant was:

> *To whatever extent* messages are significant to users, to that extent there will be engagement with the linguistic code.

But even if we adopt this interpretation and then arrive at clear definitions, how would we measure the significance of messages to users and degree of engagement with the code? So far, the maxim appears to lie outside of 'world 3 in the narrow sense', for though Brumfit may - as it were - have correctly conjectured that rainfall should be predictable in terms of changes in air density, he has provided no barometer, nor even a suggestion of how one might be constructed.

But we need not give up so easily. Brumfit's maxim stands in sharp contrast with the following quotation, taken with slight modification from a book that was the charter for the most widely promoted methodology of its day:

> A student learns [the linguistic code] not by attempting to say [what is significant to him], but by becoming familiar with structure patterns from which it will be possible to generalize [for future needs]. (Brooks 1960, p.49)

The relationship of Brooks' maxim to Popper's world 3 is identical to that of Brumfit's: neither is testable as it stands. Nevertheless, we can imagine some of the things that a believer in one of these maxims might say to a believer in the other: 'If I'm right, then P ought to succeed better than Q,' or 'If you were right, then R couldn't have happened.' Each of the single letters P, Q, and R, of course, represents a complex set of interacting conditions, but *to the extent that these terms can be specified*, the relative tenability of the two maxims can be tested. To that same extent, the maxims may be said to have a place in world 3, and even in the 'narrow' part of it.

To the extent that the two maxims are not testable because their terms are not definable and measurable, they lie outside the narrow core of world 3, but Popper would still have us examine them for circularity, internal consistency, and consistency with observations and statements that are external to them. Both pass the circularity and internal consistency tests. Brumfit's maxim is consistent with a certain amount of research, and even those who prefer Brooks' maxim can adduce a certain amount of experimental support. From Popper's point of view, apparently, it would be inappropriate to dismiss these maxims by saying that 'they are, scientifically speaking, neither true nor false, [but] entail an act of faith' (Maley 1983, p.81). For the same reasons, it would be equally inappropriate to dismiss the 'humanistic' approaches in this way.

2 Humanism

2.1 A semantic thicket

In Chapter 1, we used the word 'humanistic' without defining it. Nic Underhill 'hesitate[s] even to mention the word [in the context of language teaching], as it is so emotionally loaded and so lacking in clear definition' (1983, p.131). This writer once said something similar (Stevick 1982, p.7). In this chapter, we shall try to get at the meanings behind statements in which the words 'humanism' and 'humanistic' have been used, and to search for internal and external inconsistencies. In this way, we may hope to reduce the cognitive confusion that has surrounded these words in foreign language teaching recently, and to do so in a way that will arouse as little additional emotion as possible.

2.2 'Humanism' outside language education

Let us look first at how these terms have been employed in general discussion of philosophy and education. Then in 2.3 we will examine their use within the field of language teaching.

2.2.1 Evidence from published sources

When we want to know what particular writers in our field may have meant by a term, we can assemble and examine quotations from those writers. That is what we will do in section 2.3. But we also need to know how that term is likely to be understood by the people who are going to read the writers concerned. For this information we may turn to writers outside language teaching and, of course, to the dictionaries and encyclopedias.

Dictionary definitions for 'humanism' have included the following, taken from *The Oxford English Dictionary* (*OED*) and the *American College Dictionary* (*ACD*):

Devotion to human interests [in contrast to either divine or individual]. (*OED*)

A system of thought or action in which human interests predominate. (*ACD*)

Devotion to those studies which promote human culture; literary culture, especially ... the study of the Roman and Greek classics. (*OED*)

Devotion to the study of the humanities; the studies, principles, or culture of the Humanists. (*ACD*)

We use 'humane' in everyday contexts to mean 'disposed to treat human beings and animals with consideration and compassion' (*OED*). And *The Oxford English Dictionary* uses the phrase 'humanize or refine' as though these two words are near-synonyms.

The word 'humanism' is sometimes associated with the rejection of religion in the usual sense. This rejection is implied in *The Oxford English Dictionary*'s definition 'belief in the mere humanity of Christ', which has no counterpart among the definitions found in the *American College Dictionary*. Writing in the journal *The Humanist,* Hall and Hall (1986) say:

Let us be blunt. ... Science and religion are diametrically opposed at their deepest philosophical levels. (p.20)

Accept the supernatural and the hard work of making and testing theories becomes a pointless enterprise, along with all human-made explanations and meanings. If we allow such myths to limit the scope and uses of science, we will do so to our own peril and shame. (p.32)

This sounds very much like what we have already heard from Popper. Similarly, Paul Kurtz, a leading spokesman for the contemporary humanistic movement, in a preface titled 'The meaning of Humanism' (1973), says that: '... modern man now recognizes that the universe has no special human meaning or purpose ...' (p.5); 'Science has emancipated man from the bondage of dogmatic religious mythology ...' (ibid.), and 'Humanists share ... [a] critical [attitude toward] supernaturalistic religion ...' (p.7).

For Kurtz, '... man ... cannot look outside himself for salvation' (p.5). In this view, science and religion are mutually exclusive, each providing some sort of escape from the other. Küng (1966), on the other hand, though he speaks of '["secular"] humanism*s*' [emphasis added] in contrast to Christianity and other world religions, proposes to show that 'Christianity cannot be properly understood except as radical humanism' (p.31).

But 'humanist' is a term used to describe movements which have worked for change in areas other than religion: for example, the fifteenth-century movement in European universities to replace the relatively abstract 'seven liberal arts' (grammar, rhetoric, logic, astronomy, geometry, music) with studies concentrated on values more closely related to human beings. These studies emphasized the study of Greek and Roman writers whose works were thought to represent the highest expression of *human* nature (Butts 1964). Similarly, when the rapid development of natural science in the nineteenth century had turned attention away from humankind, scientific humanism again brought the emphasis back to the practical interests of human living (Kattsoff 1964). Kurtz gives a general description of 'humanism' as being critical of anything that 'alienates or depersonalizes', including 'ideology, bureaucracy or technology' (1973, p.6).

But humanism does not merely criticize, correct, oppose, and replace. On the positive side, again quoting Kurtz, 'Humanists' are concerned for 'the fulfilment of human potentialities and the democratic ideal of humanity as a whole' (p.7). Humanists see 'modern man [as] largely responsible for his own destiny' (p.5), and are 'committed to the method of reason as the chief means of solving problems' (p.7). Science and logical analysis are 'critical tools' for this purpose (p.5). We have already seen (in 1.3.1) that More's *Utopia* was, in this sense, a very 'humanistic' document.

2.2.2 Five emphases within humanism

The above quotations support Underhill's observation that the terms 'humane', 'humanism', and 'humanist' are used in a bewildering variety of ways. There is, however, a central meaning to which most of the other meanings can be related. This is the one found in *The Oxford English Dictionary*'s first definition for 'humane': 'characterized by such behaviour or disposition towards others as befits a [human being] in contrast to animals'. One common antonym for 'humane' is, after all, 'brutal'. This distinctively human quality may show itself in terms of one or more of at least five overlapping components:

☐ (H1) *Feelings*, including both personal emotions and esthetic appreciation. This aspect of humanism tends to reject whatever makes people feel bad, or whatever destroys or forbids esthetic enjoyment.

☐ (H2) *Social relations*. This side of humanism encourages friendship and cooperation, and opposes whatever tends to reduce them.

☐ (H3) *Responsibility*. This aspect accepts the need for public scrutiny, criticism, and correction, and disapproves of whoever or whatever denies their importance.

☐ (H4) *Intellect*, including knowledge, reason, and understanding. This aspect fights against whatever interferes with the free exercise of the mind, and is suspicious of anything that cannot be tested intellectually.

☐ (H5) *Self-actualization*, the quest for full realization of one's own deepest true qualities. This aspect believes that since conformity leads to enslavement, the pursuit of uniqueness brings about liberation.

If all these components are combined, one might say that, in the 'humanistic' view, the achievement of beauty and the realization of altruistic motives (H1 and H2) may often present problems. Any responsible approach (H3) to the solution of these problems relies on reason, science, and logical analysis (H4). Such an approach uses intuition only as a source of hypotheses to be tested, and above all is careful to exercise critical judgment, and thus to avoid any source of knowledge - religious or otherwise - that is not available to everyone. The quest for uniqueness (H5) may or may not accompany any of the other four emphases.

2.3 'Humanism' in the writings of language teachers

2.3.1 Moskowitz on 'humanism'

In the opening chapter of her book *Caring and Sharing in the Foreign Language Classroom*, titled 'All about humanistic education', Gertrude Moskowitz (1978) has devoted more pages and more explicit attention than anyone else to the meaning of the term 'humanistic' as applied to language teaching. One of her statements is that 'through the ages man has been striving to become *more human*' (p.10) [emphasis added]. This is apparently consistent with the general definition of 'humane' at which we arrived in the preceding section: 'characterized by such behavior or disposition towards others as befits a [human being] in contrast to animals'. Moskowitz further comments that 'youngsters ... [in particular] are searching for their identity and are in need of self-acceptance' and that they 'complain of feelings of isolation and detachment' (p.11). She says that '[what is called] "humanistic" education is related to [a] concern for personal development, self-acceptance, and acceptance by others, in other words, making students *more human*' (ibid.) [emphasis added]. In Moskowitz' view, the humanistic education of which she speaks 'is most directly related to ... humanistic psychology, *and* the human potential movement' (ibid.) [emphasis added]. It is not clear from context whether the word 'and' in this last sentence means that 'humanistic psychology' and 'the human potential movement' are to be taken as near-synonyms, or whether the author means to say that they are two distinct foundations of humanistic education.

But what does it mean 'to be more human', or 'to realize one's potential'? For Moskowitz, there seem to be two major emphases. The first is on feelings (H1). 'Humanistic education ... takes into consideration that learning is affected by how students feel about themselves' (p.12). It 'is concerned with educating the whole person - the intellectual and the emotional dimensions' (p.11). Moskowitz' second emphasis is on bringing out the uniqueness of each individual (H5). To be 'self-actualizing' is '[to] function to [one's fullest capacity]' (p.12). In this connection, Moskowitz quotes Carl Rogers' conviction that one should get in touch with one's 'real self', the self that underlies surface behavior. 'How can I become *myself*? Am I living in a way which is deeply satisfying to *me*, and which truly expresses *me*?' (p.13) [emphasis added]. Scovel [private communication] points out that this individualistic goal of personal development is more characteristic of Western culture than of some other important cultures of the world.

Drawing on her reading of Abraham Maslow, Moskowitz provides a list of characteristics of 'self-actualizing persons'. Such people

> experience pleasurable, awesome feelings related to everyday life;
> are creative in their approach to things;
> are natural and spontaneous rather than conforming;
>
> accept themselves and others;
> have great empathy and affection for humanity;
> are not prejudiced;
>
> have a strong sense of responsibility;
> are independent and look to themselves for their own growth;
> have a mission in life.
> (adapted from Moskowitz 1978, p.12)

How do Moskowitz' descriptions fit the meanings for 'humanism' that we found in the dictionary and in writers from outside language teaching? The first three of the nine characteristics listed above are apparently related to H1 (personal emotions and esthetic appreciation); the members of the second three are in the general area of H2 (social relations), while the last three have something to do with H3 (showing a sense of social responsibility) Largely missing from Moskowitz' account is explicit concern for intellectual understanding and the use of reason (H4), and for the intellectual side of responsibility (H3), including concern to avoid sources of knowledge that are not subject to public verification. As we have already seen, Moskowitz also emphasizes the quest for uniqueness, and for getting in touch with one's true self (H5).

2.3.2 'Humanism' in writings by other language teachers
The glosses that other writers have provided for 'humanistic' have been briefer. Medgyes (1986) cites Moskowitz, and says:

> In both [the Humanistic-Psychological Approach and the Communicative Approach], learners are seen not so much as full-time linguistic objects at whom language teaching is aimed, but rather as human individuals whose personal dignity and integrity, and the complexity of whose ideas, thoughts, needs, and sentiments, should be respected [H1, H2]. ... Foreign language teachers must contribute to the self-actualizing process ... [H5]. (1986, p.109)

Richards and Rodgers (1986), again citing Moskowitz, say that 'In sum, humanistic techniques engage the whole person, including the emotions and feelings [H1] as well as linguistic knowledge and behavioral skills' (p.114). Terrell (1982) describes 'affective-humanistic activities' as those that 'explore the students' values, ideas, opinions, goals, and feelings [H1] as well as their experiences' (p.281). Roberts (1982) speaks of 'the "humanistic/ psychological" or "whole-engagement" approach', a term that for him covers 'a range of methods and techniques which on the surface may seem unconnected', but which he says share at least two significant assumptions:

> That the affective aspects of language learning [H1] are as important as the cognitive aspects, [and therefore] the learner should be treated in some sense as a 'whole person' [H2]. (p.101)

> That the answers to language learning problems are more likely to come from psychology than from linguistics [H1, H2]. (ibid.)

Similarly, Bhanot (1983) says that 'humanistic approaches draw their inspiration from psychology rather than from other disciplines such as linguistics' [H1, H2], and that 'language learners are regarded as "whole persons" with emotional [H1] and intellectual needs' (p.361). Citing Jakobovits and Gordon (1974), Roberts (1982) mentions '[opposition to] the authoritarian teacher-centred classroom ... [H2] and [emphasis on] enhanc[ing] personal security [H1] and promot[ing] a genuine interest through a deeper engagement of the learner's whole self [H1] that is characteristic of this approach' (p.101). Scovel (1983) ties his use of 'humanism' to what Richards and Rodgers (1982) called the 'interactional view', according to which 'language [is] a vehicle for the realization of interpersonal relations and for the performance of social transactions between individuals [H2]' (p.156). Brown (1980) derives his use of the term 'humanism' largely from references to the work of Carl Rogers:

> We can see in Rogers' humanism quite a departure from the scientific analysis of Skinnerian psychology, and even from Ausubel's rationalistic theory. Rogers is not as concerned about the actual cognitive process of learning since, he feels, if the context for learning [H1, H2] is properly created, then human beings will, in fact, learn everything they need to ... [H3]. [That is, there will be no irresponsible dilettantism resulting in incomplete coverage of the subject matter.] The teacher as facilitator must therefore provide the nurturing context for learning and not see his mission as one of rather programmatically feeding students quantities of knowledge which they subsequently devour. (1980, p.77)

> [Various methods] claim to capitalize on humanistic factors in language learning. ... [They] attempt to provide the humanistic context and affective support necessary to meet the egocentric, transactional, and motivational necessities of second language acquisition. ... [In one of these methods] students and teacher join together to facilitate learning in a context of valuing and prizing each individual in the group [H1, H2]. (1980, p.116)

Brumfit (1984) likewise notes the emphasis on interpersonal relations and on fusion of the cognitive and the affective, and quotes from Maples a series of adjectives sometimes used by students in describing the personal feelings that have accompanied 'humanistic' education: 'sensitive', 'empathetic', 'loving', 'fair', and so on (H1, H2).

Rivers (1983) speaks of 'a humanistic approach [that] came to the fore during the era of progressive education under the leadership of John Dewey'. She continues:

> In the individualization movement of the 1970s, humanistic education continued its struggle for recognition of the primacy of the individual personality against deterministic behaviorist emphases [H5]. ... [Though] content is not neglected in a class that uses humanistic techniques, in an affective or humanistic [NB!] approach, students are encouraged to talk about themselves, to be open with others, and to express their feelings [H1, H2]. (1983, pp.23, 24)

Here Rivers seems to be in general agreement with the usage of other writers as they were cited above. Unlike most writers within the field of language teaching, however, she also discusses the role of the 'humanities' - of history, literature, philosophy, and the like - studies that will

> [make it possible for] young people to develop that flexibility of mind that will enable them to adapt to new circumstances and recognize new opportunities, and that will encourage creative, heuristic thinking, boldness in application, and ability to function autonomously [H4]. (p.32)

A person with this kind of education

> is open to new ideas, open to trying the untried, yet not swept away by intermittent waves of fads and superficial enthusiasms, because there is an anchor of conviction that results from understanding beliefs one has made one's own [H3, H4]. ... The foreign language teacher is essentially a *humanist* [in this sense]. (p.23) [emphasis added]

In a later chapter in the same book, Rivers suggests that this goal should replace the traditional goal of schooling language minority students - that of laying a foundation for future study.

2.4 A tentative map of the humanisms

In 2.2.2 we listed five overlapping components related to our central definition of 'humane' and, in 2.2.3, indicated very briefly how these emphases have shown up in various 'humanistic' trends within language teaching. To summarize the same observations from a slightly different perspective, in is possible to see 'humanism' primarily as:

• *Development* of the human race as a whole toward enlightenment, refinement, and greater differentiation from animals: in other words, toward its 'full potential' (H5)

or as:

• *Participation* of individuals in the above-described development or both.

Either of these kinds of 'humanism' leads toward unity - toward a shared stock of knowledge, insights, and manners.

Another view of 'humanism' encourages unlikenesses and tends toward diversity. Jakobovits and Gordon (1974) provide perhaps the clearest example of an orientation that appears not only to value diversity (H5), but even to deplore the kind of education that values unity:

> The creative potential of teachers and school administrators, of students, of legislators, and the larger community must be given a chance to unfold and flourish in an atmosphere that is free from the stifling restrictions of the philosophy of accountability. In the reality of the new consciousness, individual freedom alone can unleash man's creative energies, not coercion, not competition, not accountability, but faith, freedom, cooperation, permissiveness, trust, hope. (1974, p.97)

This quotation also illustrates some of the kinds of rhetorical devices at which we shall look in Chapter 4.

Within the field of education, 'humanism' is often thought of as emphasizing the integration of cognition and affect (treating students as 'whole persons'), possibly as a *means* toward one or another of the kinds of development mentioned in this and the preceding section. H1 (the 'feelings' component of humanism) both tends toward diversity with regard to individual emotions, and promotes unity with regard to the appreciation of art and literature. H2 and H3 (the emphases on social relations and on responsibility) are, of course, primarily unifying. Insofar as H4 (the emphasis on intellect) rejects whatever interferes with freedom of thought and creativity, it builds diversity, but insofar as it rejects what has not been subjected to public scrutiny and criticism, it preserves unity. H5 of course tends primarily toward diversity. What is called 'humanism' thus covers a rather broad range of emphases and commitments. Yet this range is not without its internal boundaries. In W.H. Auden's poem '*Horae Canonicae:* Vespers', two men pass each other on the road at dusk. One is an Arcadian, the other a Utopian. Each recognizes in the other his 'Anti-type', and the Arcadian remarks that 'between my Eden and his New Jerusalem, no treaty is negotiable'. As the Arcadian puts it:

> In my Eden a person who dislikes Bellini has the good manners not to get born: In his New Jerusalem a person who dislikes work will be very sorry he was born.

> In my Eden we have a few beam-engines, saddle-tank locomotives, overshot waterwheels and other beautiful pieces of obsolete machinery to play with: In his New Jerusalem even chefs will be cucumber-cool machine minders.

In my Eden our only source of political news is gossip: In his New Jerusalem there will be a special daily in simplified spelling for non-verbal types.

In my Eden each observes his compulsive rituals and superstitious tabus but we have no morals: In his New Jerusalem the temples will be empty but all will practise the rational virtues.

Each is, in his own way, a 'humanist'. The diversity-loving Arcadian is devoted to the pursuit of beauty, pleasure, and cordial relationships, while the unity-enforcing Utopian cares only for science, order, and disciplined intellect.

In education those who, like Carl Rogers, are most immediately concerned with helping each person to 'become that self which one truly is', may argue that pursuit of diversity will not lead to chaos because

> the basic nature of the human being, when functioning freely, is constructive and trustworthy. ...When we are able to free the individual from defensiveness, so that
> he is open to the wide range of his own needs, as well as the wide range of environmental and social demands, his reactions may be trusted to be positive, forward-moving, constructive. We do not need to ask who will socialize him, for one of his own deepest needs is for affiliation and communication with others. As he becomes more fully himself, he will become more realistically socialized. We do not need to ask who will control his aggressive impulses; for as he becomes more open to all of his impulses, his need to be liked by others and his tendency to give affection will be as strong as his impulses to strike out or to seize for himself. ... His total behavior ... will be ... behavior which is appropriate to the survival and enhancement of a highly social animal. (Rogers 1961, p.194)

Those who prefer to concentrate on the 'humanistic' building and transmission of a tradition may pursue a strategy opposite to that found in Carl Rogers' brand of humanism. They may argue, like Rivers (see 2.3.2), that only as we come to participate in tradition will we be equipped to grow into whole, well-differentiated individuals. In this view, affiliation leads to liberation, rather than liberation leading to affiliation, in Rogers' terms. In the sense indicated at the end of Chapter 1, however, the choice of either of these strategies is a matter of 'faith', for neither can be proved or falsified, and each is consistent with a different set of problems, desiderata, and values. In the poem quoted above, Auden questions whether the meeting of the Arcadian and the Utopian was 'simply a fortuitous intersection of life-paths, loyal to different fibs? Or also a rendezvous between two accomplices who, in spite of themselves, cannot resist meeting ...'. It appears that most of the techniques described by writers like Moskowitz, or Wilson and Wattenmaker, or Galyean, are primarily of the sort that increase diversity although, as Brumfit has pointed out (1982a), in the hands of a skilled teacher they may produce important by-products that strengthen unity.

Popper, at whose autobiography we looked in Chapter 1, appears to be predominately a promoter and preserver of unity. Even when he speaks of 'growing, and becoming ourselves' - a phrase reminiscent of Carl Rogers - he sees this growth as taking place through a responsible relationship to the shared intellectual objects of what he calls world 3. The same is true of Brumfit's 'defence of reason in a humanistic context' (1982a, p.17ff.), which he derives mainly from Popper. Brumfit ends his article by asking the reader to judge 'whether or not [his] approach ... can be called humanistic'. His brand of 'humanism' is more inclusive, and more representative of how that word has been used outside of language teaching, than some of the here-and-now, feeling-oriented language-teaching methods that have commonly been labeled 'humanistic'. We may agree with Brumfit (1982a, p.19) that 'whatever it is called, humanity needs it'. But it may also be that humanity can do with a few of those somewhat Arcadian methods that he seems so wary of.

2.5 The 'stance of despair', and three remedies for it

What, finally, is the human condition? Let us look at a series of four possible answers to this question. The first answer - in effect the 'default' answer - is what we might call 'the stance of despair'. In this view:

- [ ] The only purposes at work in history are those of individual human beings.
- [ ] After some thousands of years, those purposes are pretty familiar to us, and are not going to change.
- [ ] Some of those purposes are constructive, but some are ugly, and they are frequently in conflict with one another.
- [ ] Conflict is also found within individuals. All individuals have a body, a mind, and emotions, but an event may affect only the body or only the mind or only the emotions, without affecting the other two.
- [ ] Though there is constant growth in the amount of factual and technological *knowledge*, the amount of *wisdom* and *moral strength* available for guiding that knowledge is not going to increase.

The other three answers are replies to this 'stance of despair'. One is the 'secular humanistic vision'. It agrees that the only purposes and the only powers at work in history are human, but it offers sources of hope:

- ☐ Human powers are far greater than those we know of at present. We need to explore those powers so that we can make fuller use of them.
- ☐ A whole person consists of body, mind, and emotions in constant interaction with one another.
- ☐ As we come to fuller understanding of our powers of body, mind, and emotions, we will become better able to bring them into harmony with one another.
- ☐ Similarly, we can achieve greater and greater degrees of harmony within small groups, whole cultures, and the world at large.
- ☐ What is called 'wisdom' is actually a special kind of knowledge - knowledge about the workings of intra- and interpersonal life. This knowledge can be developed by applying the same rational principles that are effective in learning about geology or meteorology or epidemiology.

A second reply is the 'supernaturalistic vision'. It concurs with the 'stance of despair' regarding human limitations and conflicts, but sees these simply as evidence of our earthly or fallen nature. It has little patience with attempts to explore unfamiliar areas of human potential, or to establish harmony through the exercise of human reason. It offers a different path out of despair:

- ☐ The purposes present in history are divine as well as human.
- ☐ These divine purposes are manifestations of divine wisdom.
- ☐ They are carried out through the activity of divine power.
- ☐ Deliverance is possible only through conformity to divine purposes, and through trust in divine power.

A third reply is provided by what might be called the 'religious humanistic vision'. It combines positive elements from the secular and supernaturalistic views:

- ☐ Human powers are far greater than those we know of at present.
- ☐ Human wisdom is also capable of significant growth.
- ☐ Wise exercise of expanded powers may lead to greater harmony, both within and among people.
- ☐ Whatever human powers exist, whether present or potential, come from a divine source.

- [ ] Human wisdom, if it is to be lasting and constructive, must conform to divine wisdom.
- [ ] Both the exploration of human powers and the development of human wisdom may proceed with divine guidance, assisted by divine power.

No doubt all four of these answers come in various Arcadian and various Utopian versions. My purpose here is neither to recommend nor to reject any of them, but only to point them out. When they are stated overtly in this way, they result in enough conflict as it is. Thus, the secular humanist is likely to think that the supernaturalist is intransigent, living powerless in the darkness of ignorance, worshiping a figment of his or her own mind. The supernaturalist, in turn, may think the secular humanist is intoxicated with a little knowledge, is blinded by the Powers of Darkness, and worships his or her own mind. Each will see the religious humanist as an undeclared ally of the other, while the religious humanist thinks each of them an extremist. And whoever maintains the stance of despair will see all of the others as impractical dreamers.

But it is when these differences are not stated openly that they become most serious. If they remain covert, they may have a number of negative results: a feeling of threat, displaced anger, difficulty in hearing what one's opponents are saying, and inability to criticize one's own contributions to a discussion. Whenever deep unrecognized concerns are at stake, the need to prevail (and the dread of being prevailed over) make rhetoric more urgent than logic. Popperian rational exchange then becomes impossible.

3 Using words: metaphor

3.1 Metaphor: what it is and how it works

In Chapter 2, we saw how unnoticed variations in the use of certain key words have complicated the discussion of 'humanistic' developments in language teaching. Other obstacles to the clear formulation and criticism of 'world-3 objects' related to this topic have come from imprecise use of certain characteristic metaphors. In this chapter we shall take a close look at the most conspicuous of those metaphors, keeping in mind Popper's admonition (1.2.1) that we must be careful both with our reasoning and with our rhetoric - the full range of means that we use in order to influence one another's thought and conduct.

Metaphor is one of the most powerful of rhetorical devices. Deutsch (1974) quotes Aristotle to the effect that 'the greatest thing by far is to have a command of metaphor' (p.84). But their power sometimes makes metaphors too tempting as tools of communication, and Guiora (1983) quite properly warns against using them carelessly or letting arguments depend on them. It may therefore be worthwhile to examine this particular rhetorical device and to see how it works.

3.1.1 Some basic terminology

Deutsch (1974) describes a metaphor as: 'language that implies a relationship, of which similarity is a significant feature, between two things and so changes our apprehension of either or both' (p.84). For Deutsch, following I.A. Richards, the 'vehicle' of a metaphor is 'the figure that carries the weight of the comparison', while its 'tenor' is the subject to which the vehicle refers (p.85). So, for example, in what is perhaps the most basic of all of the metaphors in psycholinguistics, 'a black box' is the vehicle and 'the working of the mind during communication' is the tenor. Sometimes the tenor of a metaphor is unexpressed. An implied tenor may be quite clear, as in the proverb 'A stitch in time saves nine'. Shakespeare's vehicle 'Bare ruin'd choirs, where late the sweet birds sang' refers to old age, though old age - the tenor - is never mentioned in the sonnet.

We also need to remember Fowler's (1926) distinction between 'live' and 'dead' metaphors. The former are created and received with full recognition of their figurative nature, and this very fact limits the damage an inappropriate live metaphor can do. 'Dead' metaphors are those that occur so often that their users have ceased to be aware that the words which form them are not to be understood literally. Some metaphors are so dead that they can be recognized only by specialists. 'Metaphor' is Greek for 'a transfer', and 'transfer' is itself Latin for 'carry across', but for most of us the Greek and Latin words have lost that ability, which 'carry across' still has, to create mental pictures. We will not be concerned in this chapter with this kind of etymological metaphor. Fowler warns that other metaphors, while not fully 'live', are not quite 'dead' either, and may, from time to time, rise up to haunt a writer. We shall look at several of these later in this chapter.

3.1.2 Attributive and reminiscent connections: Annie Laurie's brow

For the purposes of this chapter, similes are not very different from metaphors. Technically, a metaphor only suggests a resemblance between its vehicle and its tenor, while a simile explicitly states - commonly by the use of 'like' or 'as' - that a resemblance exists. To borrow from the well-known song 'Annie Laurie':

Simile:	Her brow is like [a] snowdrift.
Metaphor:	Her brow is a snowdrift.

'Snowdrift' is, of course, the vehicle here, and Annie Laurie's brow is the tenor. But the explicitness of the statement that a resemblance exists does not make the nature of the resemblance any clearer in a simile than in a metaphor. In spite of the formal difference between them, the two are equally unlike a straightforward prose discussion of the resemblance. In an 'imagist' view of memory outlined elsewhere (Stevick 1986, p.ix) vehicle and tenor share a wide range of *attributes* or 'items', but do not share others:

> Her brow is similar to a snowdrift in that it is white, and smooth - an awe-inspiring natural phenomenon showing no signs of previous unpleasant experiences, relatively cool to the touch, and pleasant to look at. It is however dissimilar in that it is not actually cold and does not melt at temperatures above 0° Celsius, nor can fingers or sticks be easily poked into it.

What this earnest description gains in accuracy it loses in conciseness and emotional impact. It would be as deadening in poetry as a metaphor or a simile can be treacherous in reasoned discourse. But the same imagist view takes into account recalled associations (*reminiscences*) that are not actually defining qualities of the vehicle and tenor:

> I remember what a thrill it was as a child to go out in the morning after a snowfall and look at the snowdrifts. The sun was bright, the air was clean, I felt rested and invigorated from a good night's sleep, and full of optimism ...

> I remember what fun it was to jump into a new snowdrift and leave marks in it ...

> I remember going out for a sleigh-ride with Fanny Bright, and how the sleigh was upset when the horse got into a snowdrift ...

and so forth. E.L. Harris (1986, p.71) lists 'secrecy, protectiveness, deliciousness (at least initially), beauty and peacefulness' as non-defining qualities frequently associated with snow, presumably on the basis of reminiscence. Any metaphor - or any word, for that matter - carries its own set of what we may call 'attributive and reminiscent connections' (ARCs), though, of course, the precise contents of this set will vary from person to person and from occasion to occasion.

3.1.3 Metaphors as labels

As Walters and Wolf (1986) have pointed out, 'any model of reading [or of listening, EWS] must include at least two sources of information - a text [or speaker] and a reader [or hearer]' (p.48). When creating a metaphor, an originator tries to use words in such a way that receivers' minds will assemble and respond perhaps not to all of the associations in which the vehicle participates, but to a subset that will cause the receivers to construct a mental image with the impact that the originator desires.

Guiora (1972) discusses the formation of theoretical constructs. But we cannot conveniently talk about constructs without labeling them. There are at least four common kinds of labels:

1   arbitrary: e.g. 'AN/APQ-13', 'Type B'
2   acronym based on how the construct fits into a larger context: e.g. L(anguage) A(cquisition) D(evice)
3   acronym based on internal characteristics: e.g. A(ttributive) and R(eminiscent) C(onnections)
4   metaphors: e.g. 'black box', 'level'.

Though even acronyms can be arranged to come out with pleasant sounds and favorable attributive and reminiscent connections, for example, 'ARC' itself, metaphor has the rhetorical advantages of being the most entertaining and the most memorable kind of label. What metaphor adds to clarity of expression, however, it may subtract from clarity of thought.

3.1.4 Examples: two mixed metaphors

The best-known but least important danger in 'live' metaphors lies in their inadvertent mixing. In fact the study of tip-of-the-tongue and slip-of-the-tongue experiences has been of positive help to psychologists in their search for clues as to how the mind works. Similarly, mixed metaphors may cast light on the working of metaphors in general. One innocuous example is:

> [These two sets of facts] are separated by an insurmountable chasm. (Jakobovits and Gordon 1974, p.231)

Here the vehicle consists of the two words, each with its own set of attributive and reminiscent connections (ARCs):

Partial ARC for 'surmount'

Vehicle		*Tenor*
1 Climb to the top of something.		—
2 Overcome a difficulty.	*fits*	Demonstrate a relationship between two things that seem to be unrelated.
3 Strenuous exertion.	*fits*	To reason carefully.
4 Courage.		—
5 Patience.	*fits*	To reason for a long period of time.

Partial ARC for 'chasm'

1 Steep-sided depression in the earth.		—
2 Large.	*fits*	The differences between two sets of facts are many or great or both.
3 People sometimes fall into them.		—
4 Frightening.		—
5 One means by which passage from one place to another may be blocked.	*fits*	It is not feasible to compare items from the two sets, or to combine them as parts of a single line of reasoning.

To anyone for whom 'surmount' brings a picture of climbing to the top of something and crossing over it, and for whom a 'chasm' is a large, steep-sided depression in the earth, this collocation produces mild humor based on incongruity. Yet the intention is perfectly clear: the two sets of facts that the metaphor refers to are so different in their nature that no amount of intellectual exertion will make it possible for us to compare facts from different sets, or to combine them together in a single line of reasoning.

A second example of apparently inadvertent mixing is:

> Language [is] a manifestation and ... an engine of that intricate and many-colored fabric we call personality. (Guiora 1983, p.9)

Here the desired meaning is not so obvious. Perhaps the writer intended to use the live metaphor 'many-colored fabric' but did not notice the not-quite-dead metaphor in 'engine'. Except for slightly reducing the clarity of the sentence, however, this mixed metaphor seems harmless enough.

The 'snowdrift' and 'chasm' metaphors are easy to follow, partly because (1) they are live and out in the open, and partly because (2) they have been employed primarily for the purpose of 'enhanc[ing] clarity or vivacity of style' (Whately, quoted in Allibone 1876, p.469) rather than for 'illustrat[ing] more abstruse and unfamiliar ideas, which the mind is not yet thoroughly accustomed to' (Locke, ibid., p.468). Perhaps most important, (3) both the vehicle and the tenor are familiar, at least to anyone who has ever observed snowdrifts and young women's foreheads, or who has both trudged through large ditches and struggled to relate incompatible sets of facts. For all these reasons, we have little trouble in picking out the appropriate associations and ignoring the inappropriate ones. The 'engine' metaphor is more difficult, and it is the one that is, in Fowler's terms, 'dead' (or at least, more-or-less dead); moreover it is part of an attempt to 'illustrate unfamiliar ideas' and so it requires us to deal with a partially unknown tenor.

3.2 Three general metaphors in the study of language

Certain of the metaphors frequently found in the discussion of the 'humanistic' approaches are common also in the study of language learning in general. We shall look at three of the most important: 'level', 'dimension', and the 'Language Acquisition Device'.

3.2.1 'Level'

The metaphor of 'levels' has been widely used in the scientific study of language. An example is Perecman's report (1984) on her very interesting observations of an aphasic polyglot, an 80-year-old man who had learnt first German, then French, and had spoken mostly English since 1923, and whose aphasia was the result of injuries received in a car accident five years before Perecman's study took place. Perecman lists not only the usual 'phonological, morphological, syntactic, and lexical' levels (p.51), but also a 'prelinguistic conceptual' level (p.61) and an 'utterance' level (p.52), and discusses another writer's description of the 'prelinguistic' level as a 'level of transition' between 'conceptual' and 'lexical-semantic' levels (p.60).

Perecman gives examples of language mixing at various levels. At the phonological level 'When asked to translate French "la vie est dur" into English, the subject responded with something that sounded like English "door" ' (p.51). At the morphological level 'mixing is evident in the production of "[gesveldes] *Haus*" in response to a request to translate "swelled head" ' (ibid.). It is not always easy to determine which 'level' or 'levels' are involved in a given datum. Thus the author appears to suggest in the above example that she considers the 'morphological mixing' to have occurred between 'Haus' (house) and 'Haupt' (head). Yet the substitution of 'Haus' for the similar-sounding 'Haupt' is similar to the 'dur' and 'door' example of mixing at the phonological level. The form 'gesveldes' seems to be a more likely candidate. The German verb 'schwellen', like English 'swell', normally has an irregular past participle (geschwollen). In the American English phrase meaning 'conceited', however, the regular participle 'swelled' is used, and the German translation has been shaped accordingly. The difficulty of being sure which level is which shows up again when the author sees a datum as illustrating 'syntactic-level (*and arguably* semantic-level) mixing' (p.53) [emphasis added].

The metaphor of 'levels' has also been a favorite with some writers on 'humanistic' teaching of languages. For example, I used it freely in *Memory, Meaning and Method* (Stevick 1976). Because this metaphor shows up so frequently in our work, we will look at its attributive and reminiscent connections (ARCs) in some detail.

The fourth and fifth, and sixth and seventh items in the partial ARC opposite show where we must be particularly careful when we employ the 'levels' metaphor. The fifth item in the vehicle illustrates what we may call a 'discreteness implication', while the sixth illustrates a 'continuity implication', and the seventh is an example of a 'sequential implication'. The way in which writers often combine such metaphors and their

Partial ARC for 'level'

Vehicle		Tenor
1 A 'level' is a line or plane that is at 90° to the vertical. This fulfills one very basic criterion for neatness.	*fits*	Neatness is a desirable characteristic in a linguistic analysis.
2 It is possible to move from one item to another item on the same level without either following or opposing the force of gravity. *and*		—
3 Except for the effects of gravity, it is as easy to pass from level B back to level A as it was to pass from A to B.	*but*	Linguists commonly postulate that the process of generating (or comprehending) utterances proceeds through a series of 'levels' in one direction or the other.
4 If we rise slightly above a given level, we can see all of the items on that level without any of them blocking our view of any of the others.	*fits*	The items on a single linguistic 'level' are commonly mutually exclusive with one another.
5 In buildings, the levels ('floors') are distinct from one another and can readily be counted.	*fits*	Phonemes are short, few, and meaningless; morphemes are longer, much more numerous, and meaningful. The two categories are therefore quite distinct.
6 In the ocean and the atmosphere, the levels are not distinct from one another, and cannot be counted.	*but*	The number of linguistic 'levels' postulated can usually be expressed as a small whole number.
7 It is not possible to pass from one level to another without passing through all of the intervening levels.	*but*	Linguists sometimes warn that there is some degree of interaction between non-adjacent 'levels'.

implications, and mix them with other metaphors, is illustrated by Perecman's discussion:

> [According to the microgenetic approach to language and language processing], language is on a *continuum* with thought, emerging over a *series* of cognitive *levels*. In the course of this microgenesis, thought assumes more and more defined linguistic *garb*, ultimately achieving an articulatory form ... (p.58) [emphasis added].

> [Another author] describes the prelexical *level* as the *level* of transition between the conceptual *level* and the lexical-semantic *level*. (p.60) [emphasis added].

3.2.2 'Dimension'

Memory, Meaning and Method (Stevick 1976) referred frequently to 'the depth *dimension*'. The word 'dimension' also represents a metaphor (more nearly dead than 'depth', at which we shall look in 3.3.1). Probably the most frequent use of 'dimension' in everyday speech is in phrases like 'The three dimensions of this board are its length, width, and thickness', or 'What are the dimensions (i.e. the magnitudes in length, width, and height) of your room?', or 'Can dogs see in three dimensions, or only in two?' In these uses, 'dimensions' are values that may be employed in specifying shape or position, and these values are mutually exclusive with one another in the sense that only one set may apply to a given object or space at a given time.

A second and increasingly common use of the word is found in the programming of computers. Here a 'dimension' is a series of related but separate cells, each of which contains a separate value. The values again are mutually exclusive in that only one of them can be operative at a given time in the execution of a program.

Both these uses of the word 'dimension' carry a 'mutual exclusion implication', which makes this metaphor especially unsuitable for discussion of such things as emotions or purposes. In addition, 'dimension' almost inevitably carries with it a sort of 'direct variation implication', i.e. the more A happens, the more B will happen. And so the question 'What dimension?' sets the mind to looking for some further metaphor to go alongside it. In 3.3.1 we will find that the metaphor of 'depth' often has the same effect.

Partial ARC for 'dimension'

Vehicle		*Tenor*
The values in a given dimension are mutually exclusive with one another.	*but*	Simple tasks may for practical purposes be mutually exclusive, but some 'emotions' are special cases of other 'emotions', and 'purposes' are commonly nested like Chinese boxes.

3.2.3 The 'Language Acquisition Device'

A classical 'black box' is a bounded entity, the contents of which are not specified. Writers postulate 'black boxes' solely in order to have something from and to which they can draw arrows. The arrows represent the sequences in which the writers think things happen, and so they serve as practical definitions of the boxes. Perhaps the best-known 'black box' in the study of language is the 'Language Acquisition Device' (LAD). The way Glucksberg and Danks (1975) introduce this metaphor to their readers is typical of how it has been treated by many other writers:

Glucksberg and Danks (1975)	**cf. discussion in this chapter**
'[The] central feature of children's speech [is that] it is systematic and rule governed. . . . The rules . . . are not taught explicitly, [but] must somehow be inferred or discovered by everyone [in learning his/her first language].	The arrow from 'LAD' in Glucksberg and Danks' diagram leads to another box, marked 'Grammar'.
For lack of an adequate understanding of how language might be learned, a mechanism for language acquisition has been postulated. This is the Language Acquisition Device.	'a bounded entity, the contents of which are not specified'
	(the second type of label in 3.1.3 above)
'[The LAD receives input from three sources.] Input 1 is the perception of the physical and social world, and input 2 represents the speech of the people of that world. Input 3 represents the child's developing conceptual system. the LAD itself may be regarded as an integral part of that conceptual-cognitive system, *or* as a separate mechanism which can draw information from "cognition" and transmit information back.' [emphasis added]	Three arrows are drawn to the 'LAD' box.
	Uncertainty on the important issue of boundaries is shown as a single, non-rectangular box around both 'LAD' and 'Cognition', with a wavy dotted line between the two areas and two arrows crossing that line, one in either direction.
'This description cannot be taken literally. Its only purpose is to highlight the kinds of interactions and relations involved in learning to understand and speak a language.'	'This is a metaphor. Its purpose is to serve as a compact label for the above facts and relationships, and to add a bit to "clarity or vivacity of style."' (3.1.4).

The word 'device' is, of course, unfortunate in this context, since it generally refers to 'a mechanical invention or contrivance used for a specific purpose' (*World Book Encyclopedia Dictionary*) or to 'a plan or scheme' (*American College Dictionary*). In ordinary speech, something mechanical consists of bounded parts moving against one another in sequence, while inventing, contriving, planning, and scheming are all done by conscious agents. As Brown (1980) pointed out, the 'Language Acquisition Device' was first used in connection with the innateness hypothesis (the theory that the mind at birth is not a *tabula rasa*, but contains, in some form, special information about how languages work). This hypothesis was proposed as a way to account for the fact that infants learn the languages around them much more rapidly and efficiently than might be expected if they were starting from scratch. It is really just a cover term for four abilities: (1) the ability to distinguish speech sounds from other sounds in the environment; (2) the ability to organize linguistic events into various classes which can later be refined; (3) the ability to generate certain kinds of systems and the inability to generate others; (4) the ability to respond to whatever system has been generated so far, and to revise it in the direction of greater simplicity (Brown 1980). Each of these abilities can be represented as one or more arrows in Glucksberg and Danks' diagram.

3.2.4 General features of the above metaphors

There are two principles that show up repeatedly in the metaphors of 'levels', 'depth', and 'dimension', and in the implications 'discreteness', 'continuity', 'sequence' (3.2.1); 'mutual exclusion' (3.2.2), and 'direct variation' (see 3.3.1 below). The first of these principles, contained in most uses of the 'levels' and 'dimensions' metaphors, as well as in the 'continuity implication', is the existence of *boundaries*. The 'continuity implication' literally contradicts the 'discreteness implication', yet both illustrate a second theme, the principle of *linear order*. Linear order is also affirmed in the 'levels', 'depth', and 'dimension' metaphors, and in the 'sequence' and 'direct variation' implications.

Metaphors such as 'levels', 'dimension', or 'device' have status both as scientific lexicon and as rhetoric. As lexicon, they are simply convenient labels (3.1.3); their effect is to refer a reader to some body of research or other publicly available experiences. As rhetoric, however, they have an additional effect: they activate a wide range of associations derived from the everyday uses of the words. Some of these associations, as we have seen, encourage readers to think and act as though what they are talking about - language, learning, language learning, or whatever - consisted of bounded entities acting on one another in some linear order. The propositional, syllogistic style characteristically employed by western science depends on - demands - such entities. Perhaps it is the fact that these metaphors meet this demand, rather than their memorability or their contributions toward 'vivacity of style', that is the main reason why we use them so often in our field. They serve not only to label ideas, but also to shape them. They represent what is in the data, but they also project speculations as to boundedness and sequenceability. Here, perhaps, lies the danger that Guiora was warning against (3.1). This is not intended to represent a judgment as to whether bounded and sequenceable entities exist; it is only to say that certain metaphors, rather than recording the existence of such entities, only predispose us to think we see them whether or not they are actually there.

3.3 Four 'humanistic' metaphors

Let us now go on to examine four metaphors that are of particular importance in the discussion of some of the 'humanisitic' approaches: 'depth', 'the Filter', 'the Monitor', and 'permeable ego boundaries'.

3.3.1 'Depth'

This writer's *Memory, Meaning and Method* (Stevick 1976) represented a generally 'humanistic' approach to the learning and teaching of languages. The most important metaphor in that book was 'cognitive *depth*'. This concept was introduced near the close of the section on memory. It was borrowed from the writings of Fergus Craik and his associates, who had used it to express some of the findings they had derived from a series of experimental studies. In one of these studies,

> subjects were given a list of single words. About each word they were asked one of five different questions: (1) 'Is there a word present?' (2) 'Is the word printed in capitals, or in lower-case letters?' (3) 'Does it rhyme with _____?' (4) 'Is it a member of the _____category?' [e.g. 'animal', 'food'] (5) 'Does it fit into the following sentence?' Each question requires the subject to process the word at a greater 'cognitive depth' than the question that precedes it in the list. 'Cognitive depth' in this sense is defined in terms of the amount of meaning that the subject extracted from the stimulus. In this experiment, the subjects required a greater amount of time to respond to the 'deeper' questions. However, in recognition and recall tests given later, their performance was dramatically better on the words they had been given to process at a greater depth. (Stevick 1976, p.30)

This principle seemed to account for experimental results that had been reported by researchers other than Craik:

> In 1970 Lott, Lott and Walsh had varied the usual paired-associate experiment to include a factor of emotional involvement on the part of the subjects. The subjects, given a list of names of public figures, were asked to say whether they liked, disliked, or felt neutral about each one. They then learned meaningless trigrams, which were paired with the names of these people. The trigrams that they learned best were those paired with the names of people that they liked. Next were the ones associated with disliked persons. Least well learned were those that were tied to neutrally regarded figures. (op. cit. p.38)

My treatment there went on to relate the concept of 'depth' to certain methods in the field of language teaching, including Total Physical Response, Suggestopedia, and Community Language Learning, and ended with a guess that 'an increase in "communicativeness" enhances retention and improves pedagogical effectiveness to the extent that it increases the average "depth" of the experience, but only to that extent' (p.44). The metaphor of 'depth' seemed like a suitable label for such a wide variety of observations, from so many sources, that it became the leitmotif of the entire book. Now, some years later, these observations still seem to me to be of the utmost practical and theoretical importance for language teachers.

Like many other metaphors, however, 'depth' has proved treacherous. The first four of the five items in the partial ARC opposite work beautifully. The tenor of the fifth item, the 'direct-variation implication' (3.2.2), is also found in Perecman's speculation that:

> The ubiquity of language mixing suggests that language *boundaries* are poorly *delineated* in the polyglot aphasic's mental grammar. It may turn out that there is a *hierarchical* structure to the organization of the multiple languages of a polyglot such that at the lexical *level*, individual grammars are closely linked while at subsequent 'levels' of linguistic organization, the individual grammars begin to individuate *more and more*. (Perecman 1984, p.61) [emphasis added]

This fifth item in the ARC for 'depth' has a certain intuitive appeal. It is also consistent with Craik's generalization that learned material 'will be forgotten ... at a rate appropriate to its level of analysis' (Craik 1973, p.51). This conclusion implies that *there are no circumstances under which relatively 'superficial' levels of processing will lead to better results than relatively 'deep' levels of processing.*

Partial ARC for 'depth'

(Words in quotes are vehicles for still further metaphors.)

Vehicle		*Tenor*
1 Certain 'levels' lie 'beyond' certain other 'levels'.	*fits*	Certain of Craik's 'levels of processing' produced better retention than others did.
2 A continuum.	*fits*	None of the observations I summarized indicated a need to postulate discrete 'levels'.
3 Important.	*fits*	Experimental results reported by Lott *et al.*, and by many other researchers, as well as observed results of Community Language Learning and other methods, indicated that emotions played a key role in learning.
4 'Deep' things are not apparent or accessible to people who are operating on the 'surface'.	*fits*	Goals and emotions can be observed only through their outward manifestations.
5 The greater the depth, the greater the water pressure, or the obscurity, or some other variable.	*fits*	Processing at deeper levels should lead to better retention.

This implication was tested by Morris, Bransford, and Franks (1977). The experiment was summarized in Bransford (1979). In it, two groups of subjects were presented with a series of words, and about each word they had to make one or another kind of decision. Sometimes they decided whether the presented word rhymed with another word supplied by the experimenter. At other times, they had to decide whether the word would fit into some sentence: whether 'dog' would fit into 'A ____ has ears', for example. Later, one group of subjects were shown a new list, and had to decide which words in it had also been present in the original list. It turned out that the words that had been fitted into sentences were recognized more reliably than those that had been tested for rhymes. That much was exactly what would have been predicted on the basis of Craik's results. But the second group of subjects were tested in a quite different way. They were presented with a completely new set of words and were asked which of those words *rhymed* with words they had heard in the original list, and which did not. Under these conditions, the results were reversed: subjects were better at recognizing the rhyme of a word if they had originally tested if for rhyme than if they had tested it for meaning. For this purpose, at least, *less* 'depth' was better! These results were found even if the delay between learning and testing was as much as a full day.

The tenor of the fifth item in the ARC for 'depth' is thus false. Here is an example of how a metaphor, though in many ways attractive and to some extent still useful, may nevertheless be misleading.

3.3.2 The 'Filter'

In recent years, Stephen Krashen and others have made extensive use of a metaphor that they have called the 'affective filter', the 'socioaffective filter', or just the 'filter', which 'screens out' part of the available input (Dulay, Burt, and Krashen 1982, pp.46, 50, 51), or otherwise 'prevents input from being used' (Krashen and Terrell 1983, p.39). Because its action depends on social factors and it operates through emotional reactions to those factors, the 'filter' is of particular relevance to H1 (emphasis on feelings) and H2 (emphasis on social relations) (2.2.2).

As pictured by Dulay, Burt, and Krashen (1982), the filter is a box into which an arrow comes from the 'language environment' and from which a solid arrow leads to the 'organizer', with a dotted arrow going to the 'monitor' (at which we will look in 3.3.3). In their description,

> The filter is that part of the internal processing system that subconsciously screens incoming language based on what psychologists call 'affect': the learner's motives, needs, attitudes, and emotional states. The filter appears to be the first main *hurdle* that incoming *language* data must encounter before [being] processed further. It determines which target language models the learner will select [and] which parts of the language will be attended to first. (p.48) [emphasis added]

In another account, when the 'filter' is 'high', 'strong', or 'raised', fewer data reach the 'Language Acquisition Device' than when it is 'low', 'weak', or 'lowered' (Krashen 1982).

In spite of the fact that it appears as a box in the diagram, this is really a 'boundary' or 'barrier' metaphor comparable to the one we shall examine in 3.3.4. Dulay, Burt, and Krashen (1982) apparently intended the tenor to be: 'given the same language environment, differences between successful and unsuccessful learners are most plausibly accounted for by some kind of internal selective mechanism such as a filter ...' (pp.50-1). Four aspects of the vehicle, however, make it potentially misleading. One is the metaphoric 'raising' and 'lowering' of the 'filter', which always brings to my mind a picture of an inverted portcullis. Calling a 'filter' a 'hurdle' has a similar effect. But these metaphors are comparable to the 'insurmountable chasm' and 'engine of a fabric' figures discussed in 3.1.4, and are more amusing than confusing.

A more serious point is the question of just what the raising and lowering of the 'filter' depends on. Dulay, Burt, and Krashen (1982) say that 'what psychologists call "affect"' consists of 'the learner's motives, needs, attitudes, and emotional states' (p.46). This description of 'affect' is considerably broader than the definitions in the *American College Dictionary* (*Psychol.* 'feeling or emotion'), or in the *World Book Encyclopedia Dictionary* (*Psychol.* 'the felt or emotional component of a stimulus or motive to action'). To give their own meaning to the word 'affect' as these writers have done, tends to create lexical confusion in the minds of readers, and, as a result, to reduce the specificity of the 'filter' metaphor.

A still more serious matter is what the 'filter' excludes. In the Dulay, Burt, and Krashen diagram described above, the filter is the component that acts to limit intake, and it is the first thing that incoming data encounter. This sounds like a special case of Easterbrook's (1959) suggestion that 'emotional arousal acts consistently to reduce the range of cues that an organism uses, and ... the reduction in range of cue utilization influences action in ways that are either organizing or disorganizing, depending on the behavior concerned' (p.183). Easterbrook also ventures the generalization that 'cerebral competence is reduced in emotion' (p.198).

As far as it goes, Dulay, Burt, and Krashen's portrayal of the 'filter' may also be consistent with an experiment reported by Clifford and Hollin (1981), which suggested that 'observed violence triggers some ... factor [which could] cause a narrowing of attention to a limited range of information, especially at the time of coding [i.e. when it is being stored in memory]' (p.368). In another experiment (Hollin 1984), subjects viewed a non-violent episode. The period during which one of the characters in the episode was on stage was accompanied either by a sine wave tone or by white noise. Subjects were significantly less able to recall characteristics of that character under the (presumably more stressful and therefore more affect-producing) white noise condition than under the (presumably less stressful and therefore less affect-producing) sine wave condition.

Although there are obvious affinities between the Dulay, Burt, and Krashen portrayal of the 'filter' and the psychological evidence quoted above, there is at least one important difference. The data that the 'filter' admits or excludes are linguistic in nature, whereas the formulations by Easterbrook (1959), Clifford and Hollin (1981), and Hollin (1984), have to do with data of other, and possibly of all, kinds.

Another difficulty is that the role of the 'filter' in Dulay, Burt, and Krashen's diagram is not the same as the role implied by Krashen when he says that 'Those whose attitudes are not optimal for second language acquisition ... will have a high or strong Affective Filter - *even if they understand the message*, the input will not *reach* ... the Language Acquisition Device' (p.31) [emphasis added]. The diagram has the 'filter' in a liminal role; that is, it is located at the threshold of the entryway to the senses. In the quotation from Krashen, on the other hand, the 'filter' is clearly postliminal: it comes into play only after incoming data have already crossed the sensory threshold. This inconsistency makes the 'filter' metaphor even less clear. Perception may very well involve 'filtering' in both of these senses, but these authors do not distinguish between them.

With regard to its tenor, there are at least four matters that the 'filter' metaphor does not handle satisfactorily:

☐ Except in its 'postliminal' version, it does not take into account the interaction among emotions, new data, and the information that was already present in the nervous system of the learner. This is essentially the same difficulty that we will find with the 'permeable ego boundary' metaphors (3.3.4).
☐ It does not allow for the possibility that affect may also enhance or accelerate learning, as well as blocking it.
☐ It does not take account of the fact that affect may screen out non-linguistic as well as linguistic data.
☐ It does not tell us that in addition to 'raising' or 'lowering' the 'filter', emotions are themselves stored as data in the same networks as other data, both linguistic and non-linguistic.

For language teachers these four points are of practical as well as theoretical importance. But perhaps the most basic difficulty with the 'filter' metaphor is that it has been called a 'hypothesis' (Krashen 1982, p.31). From a Popperian point of view, its internally inconsistent vehicle and its dubious tenor make it difficult to understand, and virtually impossible to test.

3.3.3 The 'Monitor'

Krashen and his co-authors have built many of their contributions to language teaching theory around the 'Monitor', which is what they have called the ability to make changes in an utterance that one has already formulated. This concept stands for an important functioning of human speakers, which is particularly related to H3 (emphasis on responsible scrutiny, criticism, and correction) and H4 (emphasis on the power of the intellect) (2.2.2).

The 'Monitor' is usually presented in pictorial form, and so is really an icon as well as a metaphor. But icons carry within them many of the same dangers as metaphors. It is, however, related to the 'black-box' metaphor in that it derives its meaning from the lines that are drawn from and to it. This icon has been presented in more than one form. In Krashen (1981, p.7), it is pictured as off to one side of the line running from 'acquired competence' to 'utterance'. A dotted arrow leads from 'learned system' to a point on that line. In Krashen (1982, p.16), solid lines without arrowheads are drawn between 'learned competence (the Monitor)' to two points, one before and one after 'output'. The version in Krashen and Terrell (1983, p.30) differs only in that the two lines are dotted and have arrowheads pointing away from the Monitor. The icon in Dulay, Burt, and Krashen (1982, p.6) is more complex, with arrows running to the Monitor from the 'Organizer' (the site of acquired competence) and from the 'Filter'. Another arrow runs directly from 'Monitor' to 'Verbal Performance', but the latter may also be reached directly from the 'Organizer'. It is hard to be certain about the significance of the presence or absence of arrowheads, or of the difference between solid and dotted lines, or of a 'black box' that is positioned out by itself at the end of a single line.

What is clear is that these authors conceive of the Monitor as standing outside the main process of language production. This seems inconsistent with an 'imagist' view such as the one outlined in Stevick (1986), and with the 'parallel distributed processing' model summarized by Sampson (1987). There is no doubt that some kind of monitoring goes on during language production. What is less certain is whether this process can best be represented as a black box. Even if it can, monitoring is certainly more complicated than the icons described in the preceding paragraph.

3.3.4 'Ego boundaries' and 'varying permeability'

Another metaphor that seemed attractive during the process of writing *Memory, Meaning and Method* was borrowed from the writings of Guiora and his colleagues. In a sketch of the history of his investigations (1975, pp.43-53), Guiora explains that in the mid-1960s he was studying personality constructs, with particular attention to what he called the 'comprehending modalities'. One of these modalities was empathy, which is, of course, closely related to H1 (emphasis on feelings) and H2 (emphasis on social relations) (2.2.2). Like anyone engaged in such a study, Guiora faced two methodological problems. The first of these was a very Popperian one: how to

> submit hypotheses emerging from the clinical circumstance to a systematic and critical examination that will yield [reveal? EWS] lawful relationships between the observed phenomena, reliable and valid predictions about future events, and the results of which will lend themselves to public scrutiny. (p.44)

The second problem was 'how to operationalize and measure personality constructs in general' (ibid.). Guiora's approach to these two problems was

> to identify another realm of behavior where the phenomena first observed in the clinical situation could be assumed to exist - [a realm which] would be such as to lend itself to the manipulation of variables and populations - to rigorous empirical research. (ibid.)

For this purpose he selected two observable, measurable phenomena which he hypothesized to be counterparts of 'empathy'. One was the degree to which people are able to pick out fleeting changes in the facial expressions of patients in videotaped psychiatric interviews; this variable is called 'MME', or 'micromomentary expressions'. The second manipulable variable was the degree of accuracy with which people reproduce nonessential phonetic details in their pronunciation of foreign languages.

A series of experiments produced some very interesting results. In 1966, Guiora found significant correlation between the MME scores of subjects and the authenticity of their pronunciation. In a later experiment, he found that under certain circumstances authenticity of a single individual's pronunciation could be temporarily enhanced by a small amount of alcohol. In Guiora's interpretation of these studies, the small changes in people's faces carry emotion, and perception of emotionally-laden data can arouse anxiety in the person who perceives them. Similarly, perception of small ways in which another person's pronunciation differs from one's own speech habits may give rise to anxiety. And empathy, as Guiora had described it on the basis of clinical experience, is what '... permits an immediate apprehension of the affective experience of the other, this sensing being used by the cognitive functions to gain understanding of the other'. These results were consistent with the hypothesis that (1) 'empathy' was what enabled experimental subjects to perceive MMEs and to copy foreign pronunciation accurately, and that (2) the degree of empathy depended on the subject's ability and/or willingness to accept affectively-laden stimuli that originated with other people. Because affect is generally thought of as somehow 'deeper' than overt behavior, these conclusions fitted nicely with the concept of 'depth' (3.3.1 above) and, more generally, with 'humanistic' views of language learning. Guiora's findings were therefore incorporated into *Memory, Meaning and Method* (Stevick 1976).

The foregoing summary of Guiora's findings has avoided metaphors. Guiora himself, however, speaks of a 'language ego' and of its 'boundaries', and of varying degrees of 'permeability' or 'flexibility' or 'plasticity' of those boundaries. Terms like 'ego' are perhaps just names for 'black boxes' (3.2.3, 3.3.3), from and to which investigators have drawn lines as a means of summarizing their observations. If this is true, then the basic structure of the 'permeable ego boundaries' (PEB) cluster of metaphors is already familiar to us from 3.2.3, though there the emphasis is on the 'boundaries' rather than on the entity that is 'bounded'. The new feature is a concept to which Guiora gives the names 'permeability' or 'flexibility'. These two terms represent slightly different metaphors. Included in both is the idea that certain things are located sometimes inside and sometimes outside of a boundary, either because they can pass through the boundary with varying degrees of ease ('permeability'), or because the shape of the boundary has changed ('flexibility'). In other metaphors that we have looked at earlier in this chapter, a boundary has merely set apart two types of data or two stages in a sequence. In the PEB cluster, the 'boundary' also seems to be a 'barrier'. Whether we think of 'permeability' or of 'flexibility', a metaphoric '... is *located* inside ...' corresponds to the experimentally demonstrated '... has a measurable *effect* on ...'.

And this is where the PEB cluster of metaphors can become dangerous. For the idea of 'location' brings with it the idea of 'space', and when we think of 'space' we are likely to think of physical space. We are particularly likely to do so if we are told that 'language ego ... refers to self-representation with *physical* outlines and *firm* boundaries' (Guiora *et al.* 1975, p.45) [emphasis added]. This 'locational' reaction to the metaphors does not take into account two important matters:

☐ No one would deny that the nervous system within which phenomena like 'comprehension' or 'defense of the ego' take place exists in the three-dimensional physical space occupied by the brain. We must, however, be prepared for our descriptions of such complex activities to require a a great number of 'dimensions', in the sense described in 3.2.2. One might say that the 'physical reality' of these dimensions is neurochemical rather than simply spatial, but I have not found anywhere that Guiora explicitly indicates that this is the sense he intends.

☐ The visual stimuli that carry 'micromomentary expressions', like the sound waves that carry phonetic nuances, enter the nervous systems of all physically normal subjects to an equal extent. As Guiora would no doubt agree, the question of whether or not MMEs and details of pronunciation are picked out and used depends on something that happens within the nervous system - on how the information already present in the nervous system interacts with what has just come in. Whatever 'barriers' exist are primarily psychological rather than sensory.

It would appear, then, that the PEB cluster of metaphors is at best unnecessary. At worst, insofar as it distracts attention from the multidimensional and interactive aspects of 'ego defense', it may actually impede the progress of investigation. A new edition of *Memory, Meaning and Method* would probably still include it, but with appropriate caveats.

Another 'impermeable membrane' picture is implied in Krashen's insistence that 'learning' and 'acquisition' are separate, so that 'learning' cannot become 'acquisition'. The matter is complicated by the fact that Krashen seems sometimes to use the two words to stand for processes, but at other times to stand for products.

3.4 Summary

The use of metaphors, largely absent from the Popper's *Unended Quest*, extensively quoted in Chapter 1, has been frequent in discussions of the learning and teaching of languages. Prose that contains metaphors is often more pleasant to read and more stimulating to the imagination than it would otherwise have been. In both these ways, metaphors can have the rhetorical effect of making an argument more convincing and a model more acceptable. But the stimulation may introduce additional ideas that are not parts of the explicit 'world-3 objects', being discussed, and the pleasantness may lead readers - including the originators themselves - to be less critical of metaphors as new potential sources of imprecision. This seems particularly likely when, as in much of the discussion of 'humanism', the additional ideas have to do with matters of what I have called 'faith' (1.3.4).

4 Other aspects of the discussion of 'humanism'

4.1 Matters of form

The goal of intellectual inquiry as Popper presented it (1.2.2) is to reach sound conclusions by means of logic; in other words, by means of critical thought operating on terms that have been defined as sharply as possible. The goal of debate, on the other hand, is essentially a rhetorical one; to influence the thoughts and actions of others. Traditional formal debate is supposed to reach this goal only by means of clear presentation or refutation of logical arguments. In the everyday informal debates of politics, advertising, domestic decisions, and even science, however, minds are often changed with the help of means that do not meet Popper's criterion of 'testability' (1.2.3). In Chapter 3 we examined one of these means - metaphor - at some length. In this section we will look more briefly at certain other rhetorical features as they have been used in the discussion of foreign language teaching in general, and of 'humanistic' language teaching in particular. Then in 4.2 we will consider some of the concerns expressed by critics of these approaches.

4.1.1 Emotionally loaded vocabulary

One means of influencing thought and action is the use of emotionally loaded vocabulary. The following words were culled from the writings of several authors with a variety of views on the 'humanistic' issue in language teaching:

quaint	threat	ephemeral
fad	hot tub	moral chaos
romantic	impotent	paternalistic
purport (verb)	naïve	regimentation

An author should certainly be free to express the denotations - the dictionary meanings - that are carried by any of these words. There may be a time when each of these words is needed and quite appropriate in discussing language teaching methodology. In the ARCs (attributive and reminiscent connections, see 3.1.2) of each of these words, however, there are items which carry undesirably emotional associations. These items are not parts of the definitions of the words, but come from the occasions on which the words have often been used.

In the 'imagist' and 'constructivist' view of perception and memory (Stevick 1986), items that originated in the ARC for one word or expression may attach themselves to others in the same text, regardless of grammatical relations. For example, in the classical figure of speech called called litotes, an idea is expressed by the negation of its opposite. Perhaps the most common example of litotes in everyday speech is the expression 'Not bad!' to mean 'Good!' Logically and grammatically, the two are equivalent. Rhetorically, however, the negative elements of the ARC of a word or expression, having once been placed in a text, are free to attach themselves to other words or expressions. So, in the scholarly world, a reviewer who wished to influence readers against a book without assuming responsibility for having criticized it might say, for example, that the book is 'not insignificant' or 'not contemptible'. But negative ARCs may enter in other ways than through litotes. Thus, a review that appeared while this chapter was in preparation begins with the sentence: 'A teacher or prospective teacher who picks up ____'s book expecting to find techniques for [classroom teaching] will be disappointed.' The review is in fact favorable, and the reviewer quite possibly did not mean to reduce the sales of the book, but if one were its author, one might have a sinking feeling this opening sentence would have that effect.

In the mind of the hearer or reader, then, semantic items may have effects that are not limited by, or even consistent with, the rules of grammar. A dramatic example is Mark Twain's story of the man standing on the edge of a mob that had captured a horse thief. The man kept shouting 'Don't cut off his ears! Don't cut off his ears!' When the mob finally cut off the thief's ears, the man could honestly say 'Well, *I* didn't tell them to', yet it is unlikely the crowd would have chosen that punishment without him. The apparent 'migration' of emotionally charged items is also clearly documented by Allport and Postman in their classic study of the spread of rumors (1947). (For a summary, see Stevick 1976, p.23.)

Even aside from their ability to act independent of the rules of grammar, emotionally charged words may be used for a number of purposes. Two purposes of interest to us here are (1) to alarm the reader:

- The position or practice that I am describing with this word has certain characteristics that should cause you to fear it.

or (2) to intimidate him or her:

- On the basis of our experience with this word, you and I remember certain undesirable feelings toward the persons, positions, or practices about which it has been used in various contexts in the past; and
- I am applying this word to a certain position or practice in our field; so
- If you sympathize with that position or practice, I will have those same undesirable feelings toward you.

These are two different ways of using a reader's fears in order to influence thought or action. There is, of course, nothing wrong with these messages as such: there are times when readers *should* be warned against dangerous or objectionable aspects of various positions or practices. What is undesirable is to introduce these messages at or outside the periphery of attention, where they are not easily identified, evaluated, and dealt with.

Sometimes the use of emotionally charged vocabulary becomes indirect derogatory intimation about a person or thing. One simple example that has cropped up in the writings of more than one author is the phrase 'fringe methodology', used where it would also be possible to say that a method is 'unconventional' or that it is 'outside of the mainstream'. The English word 'fringe' often occurs in association with the word 'lunatic'. Similarly, if we speak of a 'fringe group' we commonly have in mind a group of people whose actions we judge to be extreme and socially irresponsible. Bolitho (1982) has made a similar comment on this phrase.

The exact contents of the ARC for any given word will of course vary a bit from speaker to speaker. For readers whose ARC for 'fringe' includes the above items, to say that Method X is a 'fringe method' is likely to steer them away from it without actually saying anything against it. No doubt there are groups of people within our profession who do go to extremes and act irresponsibly, and so this sort of judgment sometimes needs to be expressed. But, as we saw above, such judgments are better stated in vocabulary that is as free as possible from the kinds of associations illustrated here, and as unlikely as possible to represent implied arguments, directed at persons rather than at ideas, which increase the emotional and decrease the rational elements in a discussion. Where negative judgments need to be expressed, they can be expressed overtly and explicitly, if possible in a way that leaves them in their turn subject to disconfirmation.

Emotionally charged words combined with metaphor can be particularly dangerous. For example, I once wrote:

> So we flee back to the temples of science, to its priesthood that can feed us on reliability and validity, no matter in how small morsels ... (1976, p.106)

where I might have written:

> So we return to the universities and to the researchers who are able to provide us with studies that are statistically reliable and valid, no matter how specialized those studies may be or how unconnected they may be to one another ...

The central meaning would have been the same. But some of the words used in the original sentence carry emotional connotations for many people. The ARC of 'flee' generally includes fear, even cowardice. 'Temples' and 'priesthood' are taken from the area of religion, with full knowledge that many readers might have negative associations with religion, or at least might believe that one's religious faith and one's professional judgment should be kept separate. The words 'feed' and 'morsels' together bring to mind a feeling of condescension, and a picture of someone distributing crumbs to pigeons in a park. The word 'morsel' is one that we seldom encounter outside of fairy tales. The list could be extended. But although the writer did have a certain amount of fun with the metaphors in that sentence, and although he still stands behind the ideas that it contained, we can hardly consider it to have been a very constructive contribution to the rational discussion of language teaching.

Similarly, in an early exposition of 'humanistic' ideas, this writer said:

> [We language teachers traditionally] start out by consulting our own past experiences as teachers and learners, plus *whatever we can find out* about *apparently* relevant developments in such fields as linguistics, psychology, audio-visual technology, and foreign language teaching. We then *put together* a format ... Having done so, we *look around for* situations in which to use it. ... When ... everything goes well, a class may develop *what we like to call* 'a truly wonderful spirit ...'. [emphasis added]

This purported to be nothing but a brief description. Yet at the five points marked by italics in this quotation, it made use of subtly slighting language. The effect of this language on many readers must have been to give the impression (without actually saying so) that language teachers are usually careless and cavalier in designing and imposing methods. Of course, critics of 'humanistic' methods have also made use of comparable rhetorical devices.

4.1.2 The language of power

People are more likely to be influenced by a writer or speaker whom they associate with a powerful group in society. Membership in particular social groups can be indicated by many things, for example the way people choose to dress. This is part of the reason why some men wear blue pinstripe suits and others wear tweed sportcoats or leather jackets. We can also do things with language that will have this effect. Eliza Doolittle's achievements with English pronunciation are a well-known example.

Two devices which indicate 'group membership' are particularly common in scholarly circles. One is the use of passive constructions. Like words, and like subtle differences in the pronunciation of sounds, grammatical patterns also have ARCs. The passive is not very frequent in the language of everyday people in everyday life. To use passives one after another is a skill that is acquired only in an academic setting. To use them repeatedly therefore carries the message, 'I'm not an everyday person writing about everyday things. I'm a member of the scholarly community.' This is not to suggest that this is the only message carried by passives, or even that it is always consciously intended. It is only to suggest that this is part of their effect.

A second way of exerting power is the use of words that others may never have heard, or are likely to be unsure of. My unnecessary use of the word 'litotes' in section 4.1.1 may be an example of this, or Maley's use of 'rebarbative' in describing Gattegno's prose style. In face-to-face communication, this device is most effective if accompanied by a quick raising of one eyebrow and a slight pause, while looking at the other person to see whether he or she flinches. Words of this kind accomplish three things. (1) Like a series of passive constructions, they may identify one with the scholarly community. (2) They may leave the other person feeling ignorant, therefore humble and receptive. (3) They may also - and this is not quite the same thing - leave the other person feeling that his or her ignorance has been publicly exposed, and therefore reluctant to risk further exposure by raising questions.

4.1.3 Faulty syllogisms

When we are both enthusiastic about a position and certain of its correctness, we sometimes neglect to be critical of the arguments we use in our attempts to influence others in favor of it. This seems to have been the case with one of the points that Krashen has made in various publications. The quotation is followed by its syllogistic equivalent:

> That [a conscious] understanding [of grammar] might be helpful in some situations to some students is not in question. That it is a prerequisite for all students is patently false. Thus, any grammar-based method which purports to develop communication skills will fail with the majority of students. (Krashen and Terrell 1983, p.16)

> Some methods that develop communication skills are not based on a conscious understanding of grammar. Method X is based on a conscious understanding of grammar. Therefore Method X will fail with the majority of students.

Stated more compactly:

> Some S is not-G.
> X is G.
> Therefore X is not-S.

The same argument appears in Dulay, Burt, and Krashen (1982, p.19).

We are not here advocating a return to grammar-based methods, but only illustrating one kind of lapse in reasoning. A similar syllogistic fallacy appears in the closing sentence of a review of Lozanov's major work *Suggestology and Outlines of Suggestopedy* (1979):

> If we have learnt anything at all in the seventies, it is that the art of language teaching will benefit very little from the pseudoscience of suggestology. (Scovel 1979, p.266)

It is hard to avoid reading this statement as:

Genuine science is something that our art can learn a great deal from.	All G is L.
Suggestology is not genuine science.	S is not-G.
Therefore suggestology is not something that our art can learn a great deal from.	S is not-L.

Again, we are here looking at the structure of this syllogism, not disputing either of its premises (though its conclusion does seem dubious).

A quotation from Brumfit illustrates more than one difficulty in the use of words. In an article titled 'Some humanistic doubts about humanistic language teaching' he says:

> [My] discussion has not *related* language teaching to our deepest *impulses*. Language teaching is - numerically - a *mass movement*, and any *mass movement related* to our deepest *impulses* is to be feared and dreaded. (p.18) [emphasis added]

This statement was undoubtedly intended by its author as a straightforward expression of a reservation. Nevertheless, its effect on readers is likely to go far beyond its propositional content. Thus 'fear' and 'dread' name emotions, but they also introduce them into the discourse. The source of these emotions is represented in four ambiguous words (all definitions are taken from the *American College Dictionary*):

- [ ] 'Related' is used here in two different ways. The first sentence must mean something like 'I have not *said anything about whatever relationship exists between ...*'. The last clause might mean 'Any mass movement *that has anything at all to do with ...*'.
- [ ] 'Impulse' is either (1) 'the inciting influence of a particular feeling, mental state, etc.' or (2) '*sudden, involuntary* inclination prompting to action'. [emphasis added]
- [ ] 'Mass' can either mean simply 'involving large numbers of people', or - in the form 'masses' - it can refer to 'the great body of the common people; the working classes or lower social orders' - a powerful but ignorant, blind, and gullible herd that can be stampeded by unscrupulous leaders. By using the word 'numerically', Brumfit appears to be choosing the former meaning, but his final clause seems clearly to point toward the latter.
- [ ] 'Movement' is defined as 'a series of actions or activities directed toward a particular end', but in common usage the end is generally some sort of change in an institution: thus we would hardly speak of government, or the care of the sick as 'movements', but the 'Women's Liberation Movement' attempts to change how governments work, and the 'Hospice Movement' is concerned with establishing a new alternative for the terminally ill. In the same way, we would not really call language teaching a 'movement', though movements, such as the one called 'humanistic', do from time to time arise within it.

Using these glosses, we may paraphrase the above quotation from Brumfit as follows:

> This discussion has said nothing about how people's deepest feelings influence the ways in which they learn and teach languages.

The learning and teaching of languages involves a large number of people.

If great numbers of people set out to make changes influenced by nothing but their own sudden involuntary inclinations, society is in danger.

Few would disagree with any of these three statements. But Brumfit's conclusion seems to this writer to depend on a line of reasoning like:

- Whatever way of thinking leads great numbers of (ignorant?) people to make changes *influenced* by nothing but their own sudden involuntary *feelings and mental states* is dangerous to society. (All A is B.)
- The 'humanistic' line of thinking is one that takes into account what we know about how *feelings and mental states* may *influence* learning and teaching, and recommends that professionals make practical applications of that knowledge. (C is A$^|$.)
- Therefore the 'humanistic' line of thinking is dangerous to society. (C is B.)

In this syllogism, the terms A and A$^|$ look partly alike because some of their most conspicuous words (italicized above) are the same. Nevertheless, A and A$^|$ are different, and so the conclusion is not supported by the premises. And, of course, the negative connotations of 'impulse' and 'mass movement' are available to attach themselves to other parts of the discourse (4.1.1). In both these respects, imprecise handling of world-3 objects (1.2.1) has reduced the likelihood that readers will give serious attention to the work of the 'humanists'.

4.2 Matters of substance

Aside from the purely formal devices mentioned in Chapter 3 and in 4.1, there are some genuine concerns that have come up from time to time in discussions of the 'humanistic' approaches.

4.2.1 'Religion'

We noted in 1.1 that many in the profession seem to have viewed the 'humanistic' methods as either confirming or challenging some of their own deepest convictions and commitments. Under these circumstances, it is easy to use figurative language taken from religion: on page 58 I have already cited an example from my own work - an example generally favorable to the 'humanistic' orientations. Maley (1983) uses the same kind of language as he attempts to warn readers against uncritical acceptance of the 'humanisms': 'The approach gathers about it a *ritual* set of procedures, a *priesthood* (complete with the initiatory courses necessary to license practice) and a body of *holy writ* and *commentary*' (p.79) [emphasis added].

Writers outside of language teaching also apply this sort of terminology to ideas and institutions that they wish people to reject. The following extract is taken from a newspaper article critical of the government of Malawi: 'Private-sector development, price incentives, the magic of the marketplace - these are *articles of faith* in a development *theology* now being practiced by [various governments and agencies]. This capitalist *credo* ...' (*Washington Post*, 31 December 1986) [emphasis added]. The rhetorical force of this terminology lies in the fact that many readers in academic circles today have rejected theology, and therefore expect to find theological-type thinking either unintelligible, or worthless, or both. One possible effect of labeling ideas (government economic policies, language teaching methods, or whatever) as 'theological' is to reduce the likelihood that readers will give those ideas serious attention.

4.2.2 Rigidity

Another concern often expressed by critics of the 'humanisms' has been that these approaches are restrictive: that teachers who allow themselves to be influenced by them may find their freedom of thought and inquiry hampered by inflexible doctrines, or by social pressure from the proprietors of the approaches. That has not, however, been consistent with this writer's experience. In fact, the opposite seems to have been the case. Whatever rigidity may have existed was greatest at the outset. To be sure, the originators of the methods sometimes resisted any tendency toward modification or relaxation of their original formulations, but their resistance was largely unsuccessful.

To give a specific example, Gattegno steadfastly declined to provide Silent Way users with a teacher's manual on the grounds that they will always need to respond to situations as they arise. Similarly, the followers of Curran were never inhibited from devising their own techniques within the Counseling-Learning approach. Even Lozanov, in the case of Suggestopedia, gives firm guidelines only for initial presentation and for the famous 'concert sessions', and those procedures too are commonly altered by practitioners. Gattegno, Curran, and Lozanov were all, to this writer's certain knowledge, more concerned with their principles than with their techniques. We will discuss the work of Curran and Gattegno more fully in Chapters 5 and 6.

4.2.3 Learning as a source of stress

Proponents of 'humanistic' approaches have often attached great importance to the anxieties felt by students. This writer, for example, has occasionally spoken of students as 'laying their lives on the line' every time they open their mouths in class. Such an expression is, of course, to be interpreted as synecdoche, a figure of speech in which the whole is referred to by the name of a part, or (as in this case) a part is referred to by the name of the whole. It refers to risk to one's public image and self-concept, not necessarily to biological survival. Nevertheless, for those of us who have experienced the actual suicide of a student the figure of speech is a painfully apt one.

Some critics of the 'humanistic' approaches concede that the role of language student carries with it a certain amount of stress, but contend that the concern shown by these approaches for the emotional security of the student has been excessive. After all, these critics argue, opening one's mouth in class carries no more risk than does virtually anything else people do in public both inside and outside of language study.

It appears, then, that whatever disagreement exists between proponents and critics here is a matter of emphasis. Have the 'humanists' carried the point too far? In particular, as one critic has suggested (Maley 1983), is concern about emotional security perhaps more widespread in the United States than in Europe and other parts of the world? Are Europeans and other nationalities, he asks, simply more 'inured to the hostility of the other' (p.78)?

This last question is difficult to answer. Certainly student anxieties loom large everywhere. Buxton (1981), basing his comments on a series of interviews about the emotional side-effects of studying and using arithmetic, reports that:

> In a larger group one can practically guarantee that panic is mentioned. While I was first becoming interested in this reaction I spoke at a parents' meeting at [a local school] on the general topic of mathematics in the primary school. I asked them how they felt about mathematics, and how they would react if I made them do a test. There was general slightly nervous laughter, and the word 'panic' was offered from several quarters and agreed to by others. On occasions like this people often come up to me afterwards to pursue the point about their terror of the subject. (p.2)

Olaf Heck, an English teacher in West Germany, has reported concerning many of his own students that:

> Each member of a group of four [tutees] assured me that he or she would never go to any [conventional] school because they would not dare expose themselves. They would rather pay [for semi-private tuition] than risk anyone's noticing that they are liable to make mistakes. (Heck, private communication)

> The widespread notion about learning, especially among people without secondary or university education, [is] that learning is making mistakes and being punished for them. Even among themselves, in spite of longstanding friendship, the fear of exposure is by no means absent. (ibid.)

Heck (ibid.) also calls attention to a statement by Augustine of Hippo who, though a North African by birth, was a European by culture:

> So why did I hate the Greek language? The difficulty of learning a foreign language from scratch was what sprinkled gall over all the sweetness of Greek fiction. I understood absolutely nothing of the words, and yet I was forced, under bitter pressure and by harsh punishments, to understand them ... I had learned my mother tongue without the burdensome compulsion of oppressive teachers. Clearly, free-ranging curiosity leads to more successful learning than do pressure and fear.
> (*Confessions*, Book 1, Chapter 14)

A friend of this writer's who bought two toothbrushes in France - because she stood a fifty-fifty chance of getting the gender wrong if she asked for only one - was from Central Europe, not from the United States. The creator of the Silent Way, like Augustine of Hippo a North African by birth and European by culture, published his early works on his method in England, and his language teaching system has never been widely adopted in the United States. Suggestopedia, with its 'principle of joy and easiness' and its concern to protect its students by assigning them fictional identities, originated in a corner of Europe very little affected by American culture. This writer has given workshops for teachers in many parts of the world, but the two groups of teachers who were by far the most strongly and explicitly reluctant to expose themselves by taking part in demonstrations were in two other widely-separated parts of Europe. Student suicide is by no means limited to North America. The author of the quotation above about mathematics was Staff Inspector for Mathematics with the Inner London Education Authority. On the other hand, some of the most strongly worded reactions against this writer's suggestions on limiting stress have come from Americans.

Pending the arrival of further evidence, therefore, it is not clear that concern about stress is an important cultural difference between Europe and America.

As Heck has suggested, the important cultural difference, if there is one, may lie not in the presence of stress, but in how stress is handled. To take up Maley's expression, being 'inured' to something may mean either being 'conditioned to avoid talking about it', or being unaffected by it. Perhaps Europeans are more conditioned to avoid talking about stress, and to try to conceal what it does to them, but as the above quotations show, they may still be affected by it. In any case, 'inured' does not mean 'immune'.

4.2.4 Possible coercion and exploitation of students

Certain 'humanistic' methods place unusually great emphasis on warmth and social relationships (H1 and H2, see 2.2.2). Some of the exercises employed by those methods encourage students to verbalize - to 'share' with one another - their thoughts and feelings on a number of topics. At times, these topics are fairly personal, but proponents argue that their very immediacy and urgency allow the class to go beyond a mere quest for linguistic proficiency and to develop pride, self-confidence, and a sense of community. Proponents also point out that under these circumstances a student who feels uncomfortable always has the right to decline to participate. Brumfit (1982a) speaks for a number of critics, however, when he expresses concern that this right of silence is not always an effective one: that permission to withdraw is negated by the powerful social pressures 'humanistic' methods generate.

Like Brumfit, this writer finds such an approach to development of pride and self-image somewhat wanting in subtlety, and like Brumfit would prefer emotional involvement to be a by-product of some shared activity that has its own intrinsic interest, rather than a direct objective as seems to the the case in some of the 'humanistic' exercises. Brumfit's summary of the conditions under which 'true affective teaching' is likely to emerge (1982a, p.15ff.) is worth the attention of everyone in the profession.

4.2.5 Teaching as a 'therapeutic' activity

A related question of critics has to do with the sometimes indistinct line between teaching and therapy. This question arises particularly in regard to those varieties of 'humanism' that were designed, or at least inspired, by psychotherapists. Do such methods, Brumfit asks, in effect 'insist on public behaviour converging on a set of preconceived patterns of well-adjustment' (1982a, p.13)? The techniques of psychotherapy are powerful tools, and as such can bring about great harm as well as great benefit. If, even with the best of intentions, they are used in order to impose a set of patterns, they may subvert freedom - an intolerable cost to be set against whatever good they may do.

At the same time, however, we find such a leading 'humanist' as Moskowitz insisting on the promotion of uniqueness and diversity, not conformity (2.3.1). Similarly, Carl Rogers (2.4) evidently felt a need to reassure readers that his approach to education would not lead to the disintegration of society. And T.A. Harris, a leading exponent of Transactional Analysis, wants people to preserve their 'Child ego state', which explores data, and to have them develop and use more fully their 'Adult ego state', which records and analyzes data and regulates behavior accordingly (1967: 53 *et passim*). On balance, most of the 'humanistic' methodologies seem to tend more toward diversity than toward unity (2.4).

4.2.6 The role of the intuitive and the irrational

One characteristic of certain 'humanistic' methodologies has been their readiness - some would say their eagerness - to deal with the irrational side of students, even to make use of that side in the learning enterprise. Moreover, those methodologies tend to have been designed around intuitions - principles which have been derived from experience but which have not been subjected to rigid Popperian scrutiny. Brumfit expresses the concern of many critics when he says

> ... it is dangerous to assume that intellectual analysis and description of events can be a substitute for experience. But it is equally *dangerous to assume that experience, however sensitive, can be a substitute for analysis.* ... Perhaps before [the time of] Stalin and Hitler romantic naivety was forgivable, but the price of liberty now must be constant suspicion, and *we cannot afford to rely on intuitive experience ...* (1982a, p.18) [emphasis added]

Here, Brumfit appears to see the events of the 1930s and 1940s as a great watershed in the development of understanding about human nature. This writer does not. Although World War II may have marked the end of a certain type of optimism derived from developments in the natural sciences and the ideas of secular humanism (2.5), surely the human capacity for self-righteousness, ambition, cruelty, oppression, and mass destruction had already been well documented throughout history, and the unprecedented numbers of people who have suffered and died under twentieth-century dictatorships represent a quantitative but not a qualitative innovation.

It may be that the issue here really turns on which is more dangerous: (1) to act on intuitions that have not been thoroughly vetted by Popperian critical thinking, or (2) to act only on the basis of what has been subjected to that kind of thinking and not yet been falsified. People who would make the second choice sometimes appear to think that 'playing the believing game', as some people would say, even temporarily, is an irrevocable first step toward loss of intellectual freedom. On the other hand, those who would make the first choice seem to be saying that to accept fully the Popperian strictures on action is a first step toward slavery to our own limitations. Perhaps the natural doubters need to be willing from time to time to 'play the believing game', but, conversely, natural believers should be more ready than they often have been to 'play the doubting game'.

There are no doubt a few devisers of methods - one would not want to call them methodologists - who have spent little time in analyzing what they do. There have also been converts to one methodology or another, whether one of the 'humanistic' varieties or something else, who have uncritically accepted this or that brand of 'miracle, mystery and authority' (Stevick 1980, Chapter 22) and have become intolerant of other ways of teaching. (This writer was once such a convert to the Oral Approach.) Historically, however, any failure to engage in the analysis and mutual criticism that is the essence of professional interchange automatically limits the influence of a method-deviser, and the fanaticism of the new convert has a short half-life.

4.3 Summary

There is no question that some of the originators of unconventional methods have offered integrated sets of techniques, and shown unwillingness to see outsiders borrow or modify these until they, the originators, were satisfied that the outsiders had become at least apprentice insiders. We should not, however, too readily assume that this should be viewed as an attempt to force others to permanently surrender critical judgment and either to accept the whole package or to reject it entirely. The originators may have had other reasons for discouraging random borrowings. For one, techniques do not succeed or fail in isolation. The individual procedures of a well-integrated method supplement and support one another. As Brumfit (1982b) put it, 'the various elements are often systematically related to each other within the package' (p.193). Any one of them by itself may fail, and in failing it may give a bad name to the method from which it was borrowed. Perhaps more important, though, is the fact that each of the alternative methods is derived from and depends upon one or more *principles* which either are new or have been largely ignored in the more conventional methods. Anyone who does not learn the whole method is likely to miss (or worse, to misunderstand) those principles, and so prevent the originator and his followers from passing on the new ideas in which they have invested so much of themselves.

There is also no question that the originators of most of the half-dozen best-known alternative methods have conspicuously avoided entering into two-way intellectual exchanges about their brain-children. Their use of controlled research has often been either non-existent or defective. Perhaps some of them have believed that their most basic principles are unchallengeable and therefore not to be challenged. And various of their followers have doubtless acted as though they had found the only true light and all else was darkness. Certainly, all of these kinds of behavior are both inconsistent with Popper's standards and, from a practical point of view, precarious. Logically, criticism of this sort of behavior on the part of a writer is of course irrelevant to evaluation of the writer's ideas. Rhetorically, however, it can in practice be devastating if it seriously reduces the writer's prospective audience.

In 4.2, we examined some of the important objections that have been raised against aspects of 'humanistic' language teaching. We need, however, to draw a distinction between disproof (which is an exercise in reasoning) and dissuasion (which is an exercise in rhetoric). Each has its place, but critiques of 'humanistic' language pedagogy have sometimes neglected even to try to disprove the innovators' claims. By contrast, McNeill's (1982) article on the Silent Way, at which we will look briefly in Chapter 6, consists of a reasoned critique of ideas without any noticeable attempt at dissuasion by means of the kinds of rhetorical devices that we identified in 4.1. And Clarke's (1982) warning against 'bandwagons', cited in the Preface, is an example of how dissuasion may be overt and explicit and still be pungent and effective. Perhaps the most important point in Chapters 3 and 4 is that the more certain we are of the rightness of our arguments, the more careful we need to be about the rhetorical means we employ in order to recommend them to other people.

5 The 'humanism' of Charles A. Curran

5.1 A glimpse of Curran's approach in action

Many readers of this book will already have some familiarity with the most
conspicuous features of Counseling-Learning, and especially with
Community Language Learning, which is its application in the field of
language teaching. Even so, a concrete example may serve to sharpen the
discussion to be presented in 5.2 and 5.3.

5.1.1 Two vignettes

Counseling-Learning is one of several approaches to language teaching that
have frequently been labeled 'humanistic'. It originated with the late
Charles A. Curran, a Roman Catholic priest, who was also a professor of
Clinical Psychology at Loyola University in Chicago. This approach to
language teaching, and to education in general, was a by-product of the
courses he taught there. It has been described in a number of Curran's works,
including his book for language teachers (1976), and in Larsen-Freeman
(1986). My own experiences with it are recorded in Part III of Stevick
(1980).

Doreen and Darren are teachers who work with low intermediate students in
the same part of town. The following are only fragments taken from their 50-
minute classes.

Doreen's class

Doreen's students already know a little English. In this lesson they are
working with a dialog between a rental agent and a young couple who have
been looking at an apartment. The dialog includes the following lines:

A Well, are you going to take it? It's a magnificent apartment. You have a
   living room, bedroom, bathroom, and kitchen. The rent is very low for
   this neighborhood. It's difficult to find an apartment for only $135 a
   month.
B $135 a month? But ... that's so much money!

A   Well, if you're not interested ... I'm a busy man.
J   Wait a minute. Barbara, how about it?
B   Well, the kitchen is nice. The living room is sunny in the afternoons. It's
     not perfect, John, but it's better than living with Mother.
     (Bodman and Lanzano 1975, p.6)

a. With the students' books closed, Doreen asks questions like 'What do
you have in your kitchen?' In this way she finds out whether the students
already know words like 'kitchen', 'living room', and 'sunny'. She is fairly
sure they won't know 'magnificent', so she presents the meaning of that
word through a combination of examples and voice quality.

b. With the students' books still closed, Doreen reads the dialog aloud. Her
pronunciation is a little clearer than she might use with native speakers, and
she also slightly exaggerates the dramatization.

c. Doreen asks a few questions like: 'Where are John and Barbara?'; 'What
are they doing?' Students volunteer answers in their own words.

d. The students open their books and take turns reading aloud the sentences
of the dialog. If a student makes a serious error in pronunciation, Doreen
quietly says the word correctly, and the student repeats it after her.

e. Doreen invites the students to ask questions about anything that they do
not understand in the dialog.

f. One student, who seems to have understood the language of the dialog,
remarks 'But $135 is no much money for apartment.' Doreen responds
' "Not much money for an apartment." But this is an old book. Rents are
higher now.'

g. Students take turns at standing and reading parts in the dialog.

h. Doreen asks the students questions about their own apartments.

i. At the end of the lesson, Doreen asks 'Well, how did you like this dialog?'
A student replies 'I think it was very useful.' Doreen says 'Good! I'm glad!'

Darren's class
Darren's students are at the same level as Doreen's. The class is not using a
textbook. The students are seated in a large circle, conversing among

themselves. A tape recorder sits on a low table in the center of the circle. The microphone has a start-stop switch built into it. As each student speaks, he or she takes the microphone, switches the tape recorder on, speaks, and then switches the machine off.

If a student is not sure how to say something, he or she signals to Darren, who is standing on the outside of the circle. Darren comes and stands behind the student. The student then says, in his or her own language (which Darren understands) or in imperfect English, what he or she wants to say. (In the transcript below, these phrases are shown in italics.) Darren speaks the corresponding phrase softly into the ear of the student, and the student repeats the phrase into the microphone. In this way, the class produces a tape-recorded conversation entirely in the voices of the students. On one occasion, the tape included the following lines:

A   What shall we talk about tonight?
B   I don't know.
C   D, what did you do this week?
D   I move to new apartment.
C   *You new apartment nice?* Darren: 'Is your new apartment nice?' [C repeats] Is your new apartment nice?
D   *Yes, it have ...* [looks over shoulder at Darren] Darren: 'It has ...' D It has one bedroom and ... [looks again at Darren] *room of sofa, TV?* Darren: 'a living room'. D and a living room.
E   You like it?
D   Yes, but very much money.

a. When Darren thinks the students have produced as much conversation as they can handle for one session, he gives a signal.

b. One of the students winds the tape back and plays the conversation straight through for all to hear.

c. The conversation is played again, one phrase at a time. Darren writes the phrases on a flip chart.

d. Darren leads the class through the transcript, one word at a time. He verifies whether students have understood the meanings, and points out certain matters of grammar.

e. The students take turns reading aloud words or short phrases from the chart. Whatever they read, Darren repeats in normal, correct English. The student who read the word or phrase may or may not repeat after Darren. Darren makes no comment on the correctness or incorrectness of the student's repetition.

f. Darren invites the students to make up their own sentences using material from the chart and from what they already know. He repeats these sentences in correct English, but using the tone of voice of someone who is interested in the content of what the student has said, rather than in its linguistic form.

g. Occasionally, Darren adds a simple one-line comment or reply of his own, related to what the student has said.

h. At the end of the session, Darren asks 'Well, how was tonight's class?' A student replies 'I think it was very useful.' Darren responds 'We said things you can say outside of class?' 'Yes!' says the student.

5.1.2 Discussion of the vignettes

Darren is using Counseling-Learning, Doreen is not. Neither of these vignettes is intended as a model for readers to follow. My purpose here is only to illustrate, with comparable material, some of the differences between Counseling-Learning and a more conventional methodology. Fuller descriptions of Counseling-Learning classes can be found in the works cited in the first paragraph of 5.1.1. The most obvious feature of Darren's class is the conversational circle with the tape recorder. In Counseling-Learning, however, it is also the least essential. This is a feature that can be used without Counseling-Learning, and Counseling-Learning can certainly take place without the tape recorder or the circle.

When I began teaching English in New York City many years ago, textbooks tended to present an idealized picture of the lives of our students. The book Doreen is using was in fact a pioneer in allowing the seamy side of life to come into view. In this fragment of one dialog we see the impatience of the rental agent and hear about having to pay too much rent or else live with Mother. Counseling-Learning would say that the idealized textbooks encouraged a 'disincarnate' style of participation in the learning process, aloof from the sad, the difficult, and the unpleasant parts of life, and from the learner's own limitations. By contrast, a willingness to take life as a whole and to face its seamy side is a step toward 'incarnation'. One of the features of Counseling-Learning is that it makes it easier for students to become 'incarnate'. These theological-sounding terms have quite understandably caused a certain amount of confusion among language teachers. In 5.3 we will look at what Curran actually said about these words.

Doreen and Darren ended their class sessions with a similar question, and both received the answer 'I think it was useful'. Doreen's response to this sentence expresses first approval, and then her own feeling about what the student has said. There is, of course, nothing wrong with such a response, but it is not typical of Counseling-Learning. Darren's response lets the student know that Darren has heard and accepted what she has said. It also includes a guess as to why she may have found the class useful. The student can either confirm or correct this guess. The knower-counselor's face and voice may have conveyed his pleasure in the exchange with the student, but there was no evaluation, and no intrusion of Darren's own feelings. Darren also gives this same sort of warm, supportive, non-evaluative reflection when students talk about things that confuse them or make them angry - even when what makes them angry is something that has happened in class. He was doing this, too, when he supplied them with the language they needed during the conversation in class - including the occasions on which (as with A's and B's opening gambits) their contributions failed to provide interesting content. This sort of supportive reflection adds to the learners' sense of security.

Darren also contributes to the learners' sense of security by not confronting them. Physically, this absence of confrontation is expressed by Darren standing outside the conversation circle. Linguistically, it is present when he refrains from telling the learners what to say in the conversation, or which words to select in (e.), or from correcting errors routinely. An example of confrontation appears in Doreen's class when one of her students volunteers a remark about the low rent (f.). Doreen immediately gives her own opinion. In response to the same remark, Darren would probably have said something like 'You pay a lot more than $135, don't you?' or 'That seems very cheap, doesn't it?' before supplying information about the copyright date of the textbook.

Darren avoids assuming any initiative that he thinks the learners can handle. Physical initiative is in the hands of the students as they control the tape recorder. Linguistically, they decide what to say and when to say it in (e.) and (f.), as well as in the original conversation. Doreen, by contrast, selects the linguistic samples to be studied, asks the questions (a., c.), is the first to read the dialog aloud (b.), and routinely corrects errors (d.). This also affects the learners' sense of security. According to the Counseling-Learning model, the greater the learners' sense of security, the more easily they will be able to let themselves become 'incarnate'.

A practical advantage of 'incarnation' is that learners can then talk about what already has full and vivid meaning for at least one of them. They put more of themselves into the lesson, give it fuller attention, and so form better mental images of what the words are about. Mental images are organized not around words, and not around pictures, but around emotions and purposes. D's classmates, even though they have probably never seen D's apartment, are likely to have fuller mental images of it because of their connection with D. Words and phrases that are intimately connected with the students and their mental imagery are more likely to be retained. And only when learners have retained something can their minds work with it and build it into their system of inner resources for using the new language.

Another advantage of 'incarnation' is that it enables learners to recognize and deal with whatever is causing them trouble, whether the source of the trouble is linguistic or cross-cultural or interpersonal or personal. As these cognitive or affective difficulties are met and resolved, learners arrive at greater harmony among all aspects of their functioning, and so learn more happily and more efficiently. This is part of what Counseling-Learning means by 'redemption' - another word that has caused confusion for teachers who have heard about the model. Curran's meanings for the term will be discussed in 5.2.2.

Darren did not correct D's last sentence in the transcript. He did not do so because the sentence was intelligible and D had not asked for help. Counseling-Learning sees learners as moving back and forth in a series of five stages as far as their security is concerned:

☐ *Stage 1.* The risk-free ('embryonic' stage). Here the knower assumes responsibility for the complete linguistic and emotional security of the learner, and the learner accepts this relationship. All of the learner's language is taken from an immediate model supplied by the knower.
☐ *Stage 2.* The self-assertion ('birth') stage. The learner begins to venture out on his or her own, producing some language without an immediate model provided by the knower. Nevertheless, the learner regularly looks to the knower for verification of his or her attempts. Need for emotional support is less complete than in Stage 1.
☐ *Stage 3.* The separate existence ('happy childhood') stage. Now the learner produces language without referring to the knower either as model or for verification. In fact, the learner at this stage may ignore corrections or become annoyed by them.
☐ *Stage 4.* The reversal ('young adult') stage. The learner begins to accept

and even to welcome linguistic corrections, and also to assume some responsibility for the feelings of the knower. Transition from Stage 3 to Stage 4 is analogous to adolescence, and frequently turbulent. Not all learners make this transition successfully.

☐ *Stage 5*. The independent ('mature adult') stage. There is mutual support between learner and knower. Linguistically, this is a 'final polishing' stage.

Darren apparently guessed that D was in Stage 3 and not in Stage 4.

5.2 Two elusive concepts: 'incarnation' and 'redemption'

In Chapter 4, we have already encountered comments by Alan Maley and Christopher Brumfit on public manifestations of Counseling-Learning. John Oller (in Oller and Richard-Amato 1983) has written about it from quite a different point of view. His criticisms go straight to the heart of the system, to Curran's use of the two key terms 'incarnation' and 'redemption'. Because these two words are centrally important for an understanding of Counseling-Learning, we shall devote the largest part of this chapter to their explication. We shall try to show that Oller and others seem not to have fully understood what Curran said about 'incarnation' and 'redemption', and that even Curran himself may sometimes have moved from one meaning to another without being aware of having done so.

The words under discussion are ordinarily confined to a religious context. In reference to that context, Oller objects to what he sees as 'a sometimes explicit but more often implicit idea that [certain activities] can lead to "self-worth" or personal "wholeness".....' He says that

> this seems to place the burden of what Curran explicitly calls 'redemption' squarely on the shoulders of the language teacher, who also is in need (according to the biblical outlook) of the same work of grace. To suggest that personal 'wholeness' can be achieved through language acquisition [is] to assign to the language teacher a messianic role (a godlike status) and to invite the student to a kind of submission that is idolatrous. [I hold], following the biblical gospel, that 'redemption' (a term used by Curran and a concept implicit in the notion of attaining 'self-worth') is God's grace - Christ on the cross dying for man's sin, being buried, and rising from the dead. Language teaching, though it is a high calling ... is something other than the 'incarnation' of God (another theological metaphor used by Curran) and is something less than the 'redemptive' work of Christ. (1983, p.xii)

In his editorial introduction to the chapter by Curran, Oller represents Curran as saying that:

> The learner starts out as a creature whose incarnated existence is a poignant form of suffering which requires 'redemption.' This is achieved, even to the point of 'resurrection,' through *the knower's 'incarnation'* (i.e., becoming vulnerable to the community of learners, and possibly becoming one of them) and the progressive 'redemption' of the 'learner'. ... Although Curran insists that his theological terminology is merely a manner of speaking, [I feel] that this insistence merely conceals Curran's own godlike role in the whole discussion. [I also think] that it is expecting a bit much of French ... or what-have-you to suppose that its acquisition is a solid foundation upon which to build a sense of self-worth. (1983, p.146) [emphasis added]

One minor point. Oller calls 'incarnation' a theological 'metaphor'. But he appears to be writing from a traditional Christian point of view, and in such a view, 'incarnation' is not a metaphor, even of the etymological and inert type mentioned in 3.1.1. Literally the word means 'in(to) flesh', and refers to the idea that at one time in history the divine actually took human form. If the term were a metaphor, its vehicle and its tenor would be the same. It is better labeled as synecdoche, with 'flesh' standing for flesh, bone, breath, metabolism, and all the other attributes of a living human being.

Be that as it may, the two key terms that Oller has picked out of Counseling-Learning theory are 'incarnation' and 'redemption'. Let us begin with a summary of the ways in which those words are used in five of Curran's publications.

5.2.1 'Incarnation' as self-congruence

Curran seems to have used the word 'incarnation' in two different senses. Most frequently, 'incarnation' refers to the unity of body and mind:

> Historically, the body-mind or soma-psyche [dichotomy] ... is giving way to a sense of the unity of the person. This emerging awareness of unity suggests that all the levels which constitute a person's diverse functioning are evident in conscious and unconscious processes. It is especially applicable to learning. It might be called the 'total incarnation' aspect. (1972a, p.19)

But it was not enough that this unity existed; it must also, he believed, be recognized and accepted:

> By incarnation, in [the] psychological sense, we mean ... [the] accepting
> of self and others as unified persons functioning through all aspects of
> their emotional, instinctive and somatic selves as well as their more
> immediately conscious intellectual awareness. (1968, p.48)

Curran was saying that, whether we recognize the fact or not, body and mind
are parts of an indivisible whole. At the same time, he believed that there was
a split which exists to a greater or lesser degree within every human being.
This was a separation, even a conflict, between what he called the 'I' and the
'myself' (reminiscent of the more familiar distinction between 'superego'
and 'ego'). He said:

> There is ... a kind of continuum going from a non-incarnate state of the
> 'I' as removed from and unrelated to 'myself,' to an incarnate state in
> which the 'I' embraces and accepts the 'myself.' This leads us then to the
> concept we have called 'incarnation.' ... The 'I' first remains removed
> from and disincarnate with the 'myself.' [It] judges and communicates
> in abstraction and ideals; it resists the concrete and limited self and
> reality in which the myself must live and function. (1978, p.18)

A lack of contradiction between the 'I' and the 'myself' is what Curran
sometimes referred to as 'self-congruence'. But the obvious question is
'Aren't we dealing with two different dichotomies here: mind-body and "I-
myself"?' It may be that for Curran the body was the site of the froward
'myself'; I'm not certain. At any rate, he saw an intimate relationship
between 'incarnation' and acceptance of the 'myself':

> To enable the 'myself' to carry out what it knows, the 'I' must accept and
> understand the 'myself' and become 'incarnate' with it. When the 'I'
> becomes 'incarnate' and congruent with the 'myself' and, hence, is able
> to accept the 'myself,' the 'myself' concomitantly becomes teachable
> and cooperative. (1972a, p.98)

> In any situation ... where there is hostility in the self an incongruency
> exists and incarnation is not taking place. The term 'incarnation,' then,
> we use for that kind of bringing order out of chaos which is in the person
> himself. Incarnation occurs when we arrive at some adequate
> implementation of the acting self which the 'I' approves ... (1978, p.19)

This, then, is the first and most frequent sense in which Curran used the word
'incarnation'. In the light of the above quotations, it is hard to see much of a
connection between this and the usual Christian understanding of
'incarnation', and no obvious reason for his having attached that particular
word to this meaning.

5.2.2 'Incarnation' as the forgoing of power

There is a second sense in which Curran used the term 'incarnation'. This had to do with the forgoing of god-like attributes such as being in power, being always by definition right, and being able to avoid pain and humiliation:

> [In CLL] if a person knew ... German, [his knowledge would give him] power over those who did not know German: in other words, he is a kind of god figure in German. But ... [if he wishes to learn Spanish] he must first become 'incarnate'; that is, he must submit himself to the insecurity and anxiety of not knowing. ... Incarnation in Spanish is a terrible come-down from the divinized position in German. (1976, p.169)

> [In CLL] the remote and almost God-like figures of the native language experts, as first viewed by the learners ... gradually come to share, in the learners' eyes, the common human condition [as the experts, too, allow themselves to become learners of languages]. (1968, p.298)

We must remember that Curran's term 'god-like' here referred only to the possession of power and knowledge within the very limited area represented by the ability to use a particular skill, and that it did not mean equality with God. It did not even mean similarity to God in any sense outside this area. Maybe this point will be clearer after my comments in 5.3.2 on the Peter Sellers movie 'Heavens Above'.

This sense of 'incarnation' is also found outside the CLL setting. From his experience as a psychotherapist, Curran had noted that:

> Even in goals ... the initial urge is to avoid submitting in reality to the confines of incarnation. (1972a, p.71)

> [The] tendency in man to stay related to himself and others in a universal, intellectual mode of communication might be explained ... by saying that man has an initial urge in the direction of being infinite rather than finite. It is almost as though, in this God-project, if one cannot be totally God, at least he can be somewhere between man and God. Man does not wish to subject himself to total human experience as it really is. If he actually submits to it, he does so with resistance and even hostility. Man takes a risk and chances failure and self-defeat if he lets himself experience his finite condition. (1972a, p.67)

Yet genuine, full, internalized learning requires 'incarnation' also in this sense of submission to an outer reality that one cannot control and from which one cannot fully protect oneself:

> Resistances to grammar and pronunciation [are] similar to resistances to ethical, legal, and religious standards of conduct. Many times, deep personal reasons come forward ... which reveal [that] the person's resistance ... extends to a wide area of what he sees as the outside imposition of any authority. Yet, paradoxically, he may see too that if he wishes to learn a foreign language, be a Christian, a law-abiding citizen, etc., he must take himself in hand and submit to these demands. ... The learning process initiated here has much in it that is similar to the psychological incarnate-redemptive process ... (1968, p.297 and 1976, p.20)

> [For] internalization of knowledge [to take place], the self must invest totally. (1972b, p.4)

In Curran's thinking, the 'I-myself' sense of 'incarnation' may also have applied to this last sentence. Again, it is hard to be sure. The refusal to submit to 'incarnation' in either of these senses allows the self to hold onto an idealized picture of itself, unmarred by the actualities of the real physical world: staying in the realm of universals 'has a discarnate, uninvolved, and depersonalized quality about it. It does not involve confinement and submission to the human condition' (1972a, p.67). Perhaps at this point the two meanings of 'incarnation' come together.

5.2.3 'Redemption' as a feeling

Now let us take a look at how Curran used the other theological-sounding term 'redemption'. Here again we can distinguish two different senses, though they are closer to each other than the two senses of 'incarnation' were. The earlier of the two in his writings, and the more frequent, was 'redemption' as a feeling: 'By redemption, we mean the feeling of worth and value which a growing sense of unique self-acceptance produces' (1968, p.48). It can also be the gaining or development of that feeling: 'Psychological "redemption" [is] the gaining of a sense of worth, and meaning and security' (1968, p.97) or, put in another way, '... a movement from demeaning, disgusting attitudes to self to redemptive, respectful ones ... is part of what we mean by "redemption" ' (1978, p.19). In this first sense of 'redemption', there is no indication of external standards which the 'myself' ought to meet, or of critical judgment on the part of teacher or therapist.

5.2.4 'Redemption' in a larger sense

In a work published posthumously in 1978, Curran appears to have developed a second, though related, meaning for 'redemption':

> Redemption is ... inner approval [of the 'myself' based on what the 'I' thinks an outside authority, or 'other', might say]. (1978, p.20)

> Thirty years ago, psychology seemed to equate redemption with acceptance. We do not mean that at all. ... Redemption is a very genuine, realistic self-appraisal of what the self truly is *and can be*; and the other - the 'outsider' - helps the self become this in whatever way he can. (1978, p.23) [emphasis added]

> Redemption ... is an I-myself-other relationship whether it is in a foreign language or whatever. ... The redemptive relationship with the other ... is a very caring concerned regard for the real self, the best self. It confronts the 'myself' in those stages that are impeding the best self. (1978, p.24)

Curran often compared the role of a 'redemptive' or therapeutic 'other' to that of a dentist, who does not passively 'accept' a patient's teeth as they are, but works to make them the best they can become even at the cost of some temporary pain to the patient.

Curran also had something to say about the means of this kind of redemption. In the last quotation above, he is talking about an 'I-myself-other' relationship, and not just an 'I-myself' relationship as in the earlier quotations about 'incarnation'. He also said that: 'Somebody must redeem us *in a purely human way* by loving us and so giving us a feeling of self-meaning and worth, before we can feel loved enough to participate fully in a belief in *divine* Redemption' (1968, p.99). This last phrase is the only instance I have come across in which Curran explicitly mentioned the theological use of either of these two terms. Emphasis has been added to the original in order to indicate once again that Curran clearly believed that divine Redemption-with-a-capital-R is out of the hands of teachers or other mortal agents.

5.2.5 The relationship between 'incarnation' and 'redemption'

In *Counseling and Psychotherapy: The Pursuit of Values* (1968), Curran repeatedly emphasized that 'incarnation' of the student or client is a prerequisite for his, or her, 'redemption':

> [In the counseling therapy process, the client's] rejection of his finitude seems to decrease and he comes to have a redeeming sense of his own unique worth and potential ... (p.47)

> According to our incarnation-redemption model, as [a person] becomes more respectful and less fearful of aspects of his incarnate self, he grows more truly respectful of and loving toward himself. (p.130)

> [There is a] continuum between the fear of disorder and annihilation, at the one end, and love at the other. If then ... we are to move toward knowing how to love, we shall have to move away from the basic existential sense of worthlessness and anxiety, in the direction of a sense of being redeemed in the freedom to love. (p.98)

And to continue one of the quotations about 'incarnation' (page 80 above):

> Man takes a risk and chances failure and self-defeat if he lets himself experience his finite condition. The contradiction in this, however, is that he has no real sense of personal value and achievement unless he does so. Personal redemption - in the meaning of having acquired a sense of one's personal value and worth - only follows upon personal incarnation. (1972a, p.67)

5.2.6 Possible echoes of Carl Rogers: 'congruence' and 'redemption'

Curran was one of the early graduate students of Carl Rogers, so it is not surprising that certain similarities appear between the ideas of the two men. Roberts (1985) has taken a hard look at Rogers in a Christian perspective. While he sees certain points at which Christians may profit from some aspects of Rogers' work, he concludes that Rogers is basically a pagan whose ideas have sometimes been adopted uncritically by Christians and put into practice to the detriment both of the Gospel and of society.

Perhaps the most serious of Roberts' objections is that Rogers is interested only in helping people to achieve 'congruence' (see 5.2.1) between their actions and their beliefs or values. The therapist should avoid imposing his or her own values on the client:

> With regard to mere Rogerian congruence, there is no difference between Mother Teresa of Calcutta and Meursault, the hero of Albert Camus' novel *The Stranger*. Mother Teresa is a self-giving person, and she is both clear about that fact and 'accepts' it. That is, she does not find this self-awareness distressing. And the same is true of Meursault. He is an uncaring person who finds his mother's funeral more an annoyance to his routine than anything else. He, too, is both clear about this fact and finds nothing distressing in it. (p.28)

> [Rogers] believes that if we can just become thoroughly natural and uninhibited, we will be perfect. All distortion of ourselves, all failure to

> grow as persons, is because we listen to 'external' voices and 'authorities' rather than to the demands of our natural selves. (p.27)

> [In Rogers' view] there is no standard against which to transgress. (p.26)

> Rogers' therapy attempts ... to close [the] gap between our values and our declarations, making our selves more acceptable to ourselves. If the truth does not threaten us, it is easier to acknowledge it. (p.28)

The quotations used in illustrating Curran's first sense of 'incarnation' (5.2.1) certainly sound like what Roberts is talking about here. But Curran was far from being the kind of mere 'facilitator' who only helps people to 'get in touch with' whatever values they may have brought with them. We have already cited his 'dentist' analogy, and the first quotation on page 81 is only one place where he discusses the 'maturity and therapy of limits'. He repeatedly emphasized that there is a time for the therapist or the teacher to 'understand', but there is also a time for 'standing' - for taking a stand. He frequently paid tribute to a nun, one of his teachers in elementary school, who was apparently fairly heavy-handed in making her own rather traditional standards and values available to her pupils. Curran's focus on the learning community, rather than merely on the learning individual, is inconsistent with Roberts' description of 'the Rogerian spirit' as 'free from responsibility to others' (p.26). For all of these reasons, it would be unfair to conclude that his thinking is subject to the same criticism that Roberts makes of Rogers'.

Roberts also has some cogent things to say about Rogers in the area that Curran has called 'redemption':

> This looks suspiciously like the Christian dynamic of love: Through Christ's love God 'reconciled us to himself and gave us the ministry of reconciliation' (2 Cor. 5:18). 'We love because he first loved us' (1 John 4:19). Through the power of his empathy, the therapist is a kind of savior. By first loving us ... he sets us free from our spiritual bondage and the darkness of our self-deception, and he frees us *to love one another*. ... This similarity leads many church people to feel that the Rogerian is spiritual kin. ... But a moment's reflection will caution us against leaning too heavily on this comparison. Christian love is sacrificial. Jesus humbled himself, took up a very nasty cross, and died for our salvation. (p.25) [emphasis added]

As Roberts quotes him, Rogers is freeing people to love one another. As a priest, Curran hopes also to free them to accept the love of God (see his reference to 'divine Redemption' quoted on page 82 above).

Roberts makes this kind of 'redemption' sound as though it cost the therapeutic 'other' little or nothing: 'It is a technique that students in clinical psychology learn in graduate school. They are given lists of empathic phrases to *use on* clients and encouraged to memorize them' (ibid.) [emphasis added]. On the basis of this writer's own experiences in several weeks of training with Curran and his associates, first as student and later as a member of the staff, it is fair to say that the role of the 'counselor' is certainly not as glib or superficial as this makes Rogers' system sound. There were no 'lists' of phrases to 'use on' people. Nor was that role completely without emotional cost to the 'counselor'. Curran often described the counseling relationship as requiring a temporary 'gift of the counselor's self'.

5.2.7 'Incarnation' and 'redemption', and the humanisms

Curran sometimes quoted St. Paul on the conflict between the 'I' and the 'myself'. He also affirmed the validity of standards outside the individual person. Nevertheless, Counseling-Learning theory as we have seen it in this chapter is clearly an example of the secular humanistic vision (2.5). The references to conventional theology are analogies: 'God voluntarily gave up the power that he had, and in Counseling-Learning teachers voluntarily give up the power that they have', and so on.

Counseling-Learning had its beginning with Curran not as a teacher of foreign languages, but as a learner. He was struck by the similarities between his own reactions in that new role, and the reactions of the clients with whom he and his students worked as psychological counselors. As a clinical psychologist, Curran believed that there is no qualitative boundary between people who consider themselves - or are considered by society - to be emotionally 'troubled', 'ill', or 'in need of help', and those who are experiencing various degrees of stress in some specific situation such as language learning. Also, as a priest, he must have believed that the religion to which he had committed himself was applicable to all parts of life, to education as well as to therapy in the usual sense. These are the two central articles of 'faith' around which the practice of Counseling-Learning is organized.

Not as central as these, but still near the center of Counseling-Learning, is a tension between two other articles of faith, one derived from counseling practice and the other from Christian doctrine: that emotional security is a prerequisite for efficient learning, but that one must be ready to give up one's life in order to find true life. The reader will have recognized in the above discussion a certain discomfort with Curran's choice of the terms 'incarnation' and 'redemption'. Perhaps they came out of a process that he did not live to complete, an attempt to integrate his experiences as priest, clinician, and educational innovator.

5.3 'Incarnation' and 'redemption': a traditional view

Some years after my initial training under Curran, I realized that the ideas that had come into my head as I listened to him were not identical with the ones he had been struggling to communicate. The terminology, the setting (everyone else in the group was a church employee), and my own background seem to have worked together to activate some of the thought-patterns that I had brought with me out of my pre-existing ideas of Christianity.

To the best of my knowledge, the original meaning of 'incarnation', and the meaning to which I was expecting other uses of the word to relate, is the one described in the second chapter of Paul's letter to the Philippians:

> ... who, being in the form of God, thought it not robbery to be equal with God: but made himself of no reputation, and took upon him the form of a servant, and was made in the likeness of men: and being found in fashion as a man, he humbled himself, and became obedient unto death ...
> (Phil. 2: 6-8)

But this description is not obviously compatible with the first of the two meanings for 'incarnation' documented in 5.2.1 - the achievement of congruency between the 'I' and the 'myself'.

Similarly, Oller (Oller and Richard-Amato 1983) is probably consistent with Christian tradition when he says that ' "redemption"... is [through] God's grace - Christ on the cross dying for man's sin, being buried, and rising from the dead' (p.xii). The details of the doctrine of 'redemption' may be understood variously by various Christians, but surely it refers to some kind of rescue from a disastrous end that would otherwise have been inevitable. To use the word 'redemption', even in a sense that has clearly been labeled non-religious, to stand for a feeling or for the achievement of a feeling, will strike some people as incongruous. Accordingly, in the remainder of this chapter I shall try to outline a use of the words 'incarnation' and 'redemption' which applies in the field of language teaching, but which is, at least in a limited way, consistent with the traditional understanding of those terms. It is derived from what I *thought* Curran was saying, rather than from his position as described in 5.2.

5.3.1 Some background

Curran's literary heirs (Jennybelle Rardin, Dan Tranel, Bernard Green, and others) would almost certainly agree with Oller (Oller and Richard-Amato 1983) that Curran's use of the terms that Oller discussed was figurative, and that the analogy behind the figures of speech was only partial. I also agree, at least up to a point. But from the point of view that will be developed in the remainder of this chapter, there is more to it. This will require some explanation.

To begin with, on various levels we experience our lives as configurations. On the physical level, we are configurations of atoms and molecules; on the medical level we are configurations of tissues and organs; on the personal level we are configurations of memories, skills, reputations, and values. Although these configurations change with time, this change is slow enough to give them a certain degree of stability. The part that persists is what we tend to think of as 'us'. Disruption of the physical configuration can bring physical illness or even death, and disruption at the personal level can likewise bring its own kind of destruction. Because we dislike illness and fear death - emotional and intellectual as well as physical - we generally do all that we can to keep our particular set of configurations from being disrupted. According to the story in Genesis 3, the warning about death was what at first kept Adam in line, and the false claim that this warning was empty was what opened the way to disobedience.

But centering on self and preoccupation with self-preservation leads to a desire for immortality and for the feeling that one is good, wise, and powerful. (Hence the attractiveness of the promises that 'You will not die' and 'You will be like God' in Genesis 3: 4-5.) According to Christian doctrine as I understand it, this desire places one in conflict with, rebellion against, and alienation from that which is truly everlasting, good, wise, and powerful, even though that conflict, rebellion, and alienation are contrary to the long-term interests of the one who is being self-centered and rebellious. This is the original sin for which the Genesis story tells us Adam and Eve were expelled from the Garden, and which placed them and their descendants in need of 'redemption'.

Faced with the discrepancy between one's own selfishness, weakness, and sin on the one hand and perfect love, power, and goodness on the other, a common reaction is to cling all the more determinedly to whatever partial knowledge, strength, and virtue one already has, and even to try to develop them more fully. (From the point of view of religious orthodoxy, this is what 'secular humanists' strive to do.) But in the long run, says Christianity, this only leads to deeper rebellion and further alienation, and to a lengthening list of acts that may bring punishment. Here is a vicious spiral that can lead only to physical and spiritual death.

How can this spiral be broken? Traditional Christian doctrine seems to say that those already within it *cannot* break it. But suppose (to put things abstractly for a moment) that the perfectly good, perfectly wise, and perfectly powerful were voluntarily to put aside its godlike qualities, including most especially its invulnerability, and were to enter the world of the imperfect and mortal? And suppose that it were to allow itself to become subject to all kinds of temptations? In its responses to temptations, it would, of course, provide an example of flawless conduct. But suppose further that it made itself subject not only to temptation, but even to death at the hands of the weak and the wrong? To the desperate and rebellious creature the experience of being so treated could bring - in a way that no one seems fully to understand - a sense of somehow having been put right with the perfect and all-powerful, and of having been given a fresh start. Not least, for those who fully comprehended what it had done for them, the perfect and all-powerful would, by accepting and surviving death, remove the fear of death and the need to clutch so desperately at past accumulations of knowledge, strength, and virtue. It would thus have broken - at a great price which only it could have paid - the downward spiral of alienation and destruction, and opened - to those who accepted it - the way for development of new lives which would be more consistent with itself.

Readers may have recognized that these last few paragraphs have been trying to sketch, somewhat in the manner of Lewis (1943), an understanding of at least one aspect of a fairly standard view of 'incarnation' and 'redemption' in the sense in which those words are commonly used in Christian theology. Before we talk about the same words in Curran's model of education, let's make a brief detour to the movies.

5.3.2 A human parable, and how it applies to Counseling-Learning

There was a film that came out many years ago called *'Heavens Above'*, starring Peter Sellers. It is fairly enjoyable and still shows up now and then on the reruns. In it, Sellers plays a Christian minister who is sent to a church in an English city called Orbiston Parva (an apparent translation of 'Microcosm'). Many of the events in the movie are simple, homely parodies - parodies, not replications - of events in the life of Christ, all jumbled up and out of chronological order. When he enters the city for the first time, it is on the humblest mode of transportation currently available, which in the 1960s was a garbage truck. On his way to an evening meeting at the church, he falls into an open grave and climbs out again. His first follower, who is from a relatively unacceptable part of society, is named Matthew. At first, his single-minded devotion to God's truth as he understands it brings him enthusiastic acceptance by the general population, but later it gets him into trouble, with them as well as with the governmental and religious authorities of his day. He even ascends into the heavens - in the first space vehicle!

So far, this is just comedy, and the very preposterousness of it probably keeps it from sacrilege. Nevertheless, the film ends with the minister voluntarily giving his life in place of another man, and as he takes the final, irreversible step he traces with his hand the shape of the Cross. Although he is some sort of follower of Christ and a partial imitator, Christians certainly would not see him as a Christ-figure, for he is weak and imperfect, and when he gives his life it is for only one other person, and only to prolong that other person's physical life. But he is (at least in this interpretation of the film) drawing both his example and his courage from what he believed had been done for him 2,000 years earlier. Though he is very much an earthen vessel, the treasure that he carries is authentic. Perhaps when people found out what he had done, they were able to understand a bit more easily and accept a bit more readily the essential point of the gospel he had tried to preach. For this reason we may class *'Heavens Above'* as a religious movie, and not just as a movie about religion.

Now back to Curran. The people in a language classroom - teacher and students alike - are human beings. They have all the abilities, strengths, and virtues of human beings, but they also display the full range of human weaknesses, imperfections, insecurities, and pride. They seek to hold on to whatever they have accumulated in the way of physical security, social acceptance, prestige, and self-concept. The teacher has his or her knowledge and personal control of the language which, while perhaps far short of an educated native speaker, are still absolute from the students' point of view. This is a kind of omniscience. As far as the students know, the teacher never makes a mistake of language: linguistically this amounts to perfect goodness. In addition, the teacher is the students' day-to-day evaluator and final judge. And while the teacher judges the students, they have no real power against the teacher. Society allows - in some cultures even expects - the professor to be distant and non-incarnate. Invulnerability! In all of these respects, the position of teacher is one which is highly suited to the human tendency toward self-deification - what some writers, including Curran, have called a 'god-project'.

Superficially, the position of the students is just the opposite of the teacher's: the teacher knows all, where they know nothing; the teacher never makes a mistake, while their every word is subject to judgment; they may flunk out, but the teacher will be there again next semester. On a deeper level, however, they are no more and no less human than their teacher. The only difference lies in which shreds of knowledge, virtue, and power they cling to in their efforts at self-preservation: pronunciation that keeps them sounding like themselves and like one another; negative stereotypes of the foreign culture, which give them a feeling of solidarity with one another and with their native society; a tacit agreement not to exceed the group norm, and to punish those who do; the attempt to be defiant and yet survive. 'I have power; I already know everything (that's worth knowing linguistically); I'm already the kind of person (linguistically and culturally) that I ought to be.' They grasp for omnipotence, omniscience, goodness - the 'god-project' again, this time on the part of the students! Very much in this vein, Larson and Smalley (1984) have explored the deep sense of 'alienation' felt by anyone in contact with another culture or language, and the decisions that he or she must face in responding to it.

5.3.3 Curran on the 'god-project'

Curran seems to have been saying two things about this god-project. First, it depends on (or consists of) an attempt to keep oneself non-incarnate - to deny one's finiteness, imperfections, and vulnerability. In the learning of languages it may lead to holding back, more or less deliberately, on one's efforts. It may lead to refusing, again more or less consciously, to accept high standards for one's use of the language. Perhaps most serious, it may lead to closing oneself off from the teacher-knower and from the esthetic and emotional, as well as the intellectual, aspects of the language and its speakers.

The second thing Curran said about the god-project was that it is, in the long run, hopeless and self-defeating because it only perpetuates and deepens the chasm between the imperfect ones and the perfect one, and leads at last to death. Linguistically, this means that 'non-incarnate' students complete their semesters of study with poor accents or little feel for the language, or with negative feelings toward themselves, their teachers, the language and the culture, or with some combination of these.

Curran says that the best kind of learning is that in which the learners lay aside all the defenses that they have put into their god-projects, open themselves to the knower and what the knower has for them, and let the new knowledge and skills grow within them. All of this, of course, depends on the security that is offered by the knower, most conspicuously in what Curran called Stage 1, but also at least through Stages 2 and 3 (5.1.2). To the extent that the learners do actually lay aside their god-projects and open themselves, the new is integrated with each learner's entire system of values, so that there is a minimum of conflict and judgment within the learner. The judgmental relationship with its frequent by-products of coercion and resentment is replaced by one of loving acceptance and willing discipleship. 'Discipleship' here is to be understood partially in the light of Curran's oft-repeated maxim that 'learning is persons' and depends on personal relationships, but the 'disciple's' submission is to the externally-based demands of the foreign language (1968, p.297) rather than to the person of the knower. This kind of 'redemption' in the academic setting requires the 'incarnation' not of the 'godlike' knower, but of the learner.

5.3.4 'Incarnation' of the knower

But Counseling-Learning also concerns itself with certain aspects of the 'incarnation' of the knower: giving up the privilege of imposing a predetermined corpus or curriculum on the learners; forgoing the power of flat-out confrontational correction of errors; refusing the luxury of being able to make everyone else feel inferior and uncomfortable. In these aspects, the teacher voluntarily renounces the status of omnipotent ruler and judge. But there is one more aspect which many commentators have overlooked; I overlooked it until Dan Tranel pointed it out to me after he had read the first draft of Chapter 8 of *Memory, Meaning and Method*. This is the time in the reflection phase in which the students talk about their reactions to whatever has happened in the class. The purpose here is primarily for the students to understand what is going on inside themselves during the learning process; it is not to critique the teacher. Nevertheless, these reactions inevitably touch on the activities, the techniques, and the conduct of the teacher. In this phase the teacher is expected to give the students warm, supportive, non-critical understanding, and to do so without defending him or herself from the students by such expedients as giving them new information or attempting to answer their objections.

Sometimes the reactions of the students during this phase are appreciative and enthusiastic, and provide a real boost for the teacher's ego. Anyone who has ever been a teacher working within these ground rules can testify, however, that student reactions can also be quite critical, negative, angry, and even personal. Worst of all, these unfavorable reactions are sometimes undeniably correct! Such reactions are uncomfortable for the teacher, and they can severely abrade, if not destroy, the teacher's self-image. This can happen even when the teacher is able to remain aware that some of what is being overtly thrown at him or her by a critical student may be coming basically out of conflicts within that student's own learning self. Although this kind of experience lacks the comprehensiveness and the finality of what we know as physical death, it can still be, for the knower, a kind of psychological and personal 'death'. At best, this psychological 'death' leads the knower-teacher to give up some old configurations (some of the old life) and to find new and better ones (enter into new life). At worst, the knower is defeated and destroyed as a teacher. The risk to the 'incarnate' knower is genuine here.

The same kind of thing can happen outside the actual classroom to anyone who espouses these ideas. Apparently Curran's stand led to a continuing strained relationship with many of his colleagues. This writer's own commitment to exploration of the kinds of things described in *Teaching Languages: A Way and Ways* led to favorable reactions on the part of some people, but to innuendo, bitterness, and occasional invective on the part of other figures in the profession, some of them highly respected. It also led to implacable opposition from some key supervisees and other colleagues at work, which made the last few years on the job more stressful and less productive than they might otherwise have been. Unless one is moving frequently from one relatively brief training workshop to another, one cannot readily 'shake from one's sandals the dust' of unfavorable reception.

Then why should the knower incur such a risk? Because it is at this point in the reflection phase when the student's output comes from the deepest level within the student. However, it is also here that the student knows that what he or she says has the greatest potential for producing negative reactions from the teacher. Yet the social 'sinner' (who 'sins' by criticizing the course and even the teacher) is treated with the same understanding and loving acceptance as that with which the linguistic 'sinner' (who 'sins' by using bad pronunciation or grammar) was treated in the earlier phases of the Counseling-Learning cycle. Moreover, this treatment comes from the hands of one who is (with regard to the subject matter of the course) perfect, and who might at any time have called in the authority of the school system to stifle or punish dissent, but who instead willingly accepts a measure of personal and social 'death' at the hands of critical learners.

We know empirically that the effect of this crucial part of the reflection phase of Counseling-Learning is not merely to provide the teacher with more-or-less welcome, more-or-less helpful feedback. The 'counseling' aspect of the exchange also helps the learners to recognize and to deal with conflicts both within and among themselves. This experience reduces alienation and promotes healing among and within all of the people in the classroom, and is on this limited and human scale therefore emotionally 'redemptive'. In addition, this emotional 'redemption' leaves the learners more prepared to drop their self-defeating defenses, and to open themselves more fully to the knower and to the subject matter that the knower represents. This kind of 'incarnation' on the part of the learner leads in turn to academic 'redemption'. The spiral has been reversed. But it all begins with the willingness of the obvious 'god figure' in the classroom to renounce his or her 'godlike' powers and to become 'incarnate' even to the point of risking a certain kind of 'death'.

Once again, I do not mean that in assuming this role the teacher is supposedly rising to the level of God in order to take proper responsibility for lesser mortals and to Redeem them with a capital R, any more than Paul was placing himself on a par with Christ when he said that 'I am made all things to all men that *I might by all means save* some' (1 Cor. 9:22) [emphasis added]. To use New Testament language once more, it is at most a matter of 'let[ting] your light so shine before men, that they may ... glorify your Father' (Matt. 5:16), or of contributing toward '[saving] a soul from death' as in James 5:20, always in the limited, earthen-vessel way of the Peter Sellers character.

Incidentally, Oller (in Oller and Richard-Amato 1983) mentioned what he perceived as Curran's 'godlike' role in the discussion. It is true that within the context of the Counseling-Learning Institutes that I attended, staff members tended to take whatever Curran said and to try to understand it without criticizing it or arguing with him. At the same time, it seemed clear that everyone realized that Curran was just another human being with his own share of human foibles, and that their apparently uncritical attitude was motivated more by a desire to learn from what he had to say than it was by reverence. So this particular remark of Oller's was not consistent with my experience of Curran.

5.3.5 Some related points

Sections 5.2, and 5.3.1 to 5.3.4, have been a response to Oller's brief editorial comments. There are, however, a few related points which probably should not be omitted.

One point has to do with a notable reality of the existing educational system. Academic 'justification' (getting an 'A' on one's report card) is certainly possible through 'works' (diligent study and the giving of correct answers), but Curran never used this terminology, and it would be misleading to try to tie it into his discussion of 'redemption' and 'incarnation'. Curran did point out, however, that a person can get an 'A' but still come out hating the course and unwilling to use the language.

A second point has to do with the transition between what Curran called Stage 3 (the separate existence stage) and what he called Stage 4 (the reversal stage) (5.1.2). It is relatively easy for most learners to enjoy the warm, supportive, non-judgmental aspects of Stage 1, and to become venturesome and even self-confident in Stages 2 and 3. These three stages do not require the learner to face his or her own shortcomings relative to the perfect competence of the knower, or to become a real speaker of the language in a relationship of what Curran called 'discipleship'. Many learners fail to make this transition at all, and those who do make it often find it turbulent.

The third and final point is really just a reiteration of something already said in Chapter 4. What happens in a language classroom is not all there is to life, but neither is it separate from or outside of life. It is just one more part *of* life. Whatever is true for life in general therefore should be true in language study.

5.3.6   Symbol, sign, and sacrament

The work of the teacher who is following the Counseling-Learning model is not a faint carbon copy of the work of Christ, nor is the 'incarnation-redemption' cycle of Counseling-Learning supposed to be a scale model of Christian theology. Like the Peter Sellers character in the movie, the language teacher is weak and imperfect - an earthen vessel - and whatever classroom events are reminiscent of the Christian salvation story are pale, fragmentary, and often out of chronological order. Yet some teachers will still draw both example and courage from that story, and hope that some of what happens in such a class will not only improve the learners' linguistic competence, but will also make the story itself more credible and more acceptable to them.

The 'incarnation' figure of speech in Counseling-Learning carries a complex and powerful set of meanings:

☐   The teacher voluntarily gives up some of the safeguards that are provided by most other teaching styles. These safeguards relate to the teacher's apparent power, infallibility, and goodness within the area of the course.

☐   By giving up those safeguards, the teacher knowingly becomes subject to student reactions that he or she might otherwise not have to face.

☐   The teacher is aware that those reactions may bring about the partial or complete destruction of his or her internal self-image, or external reputation, or both.

☐   Having given up the safeguards, the teacher is in a better position to understand the situation of the students.

☐   This action on the part of the teacher helps the students to break out of their own self-defeating modes of behavior.

Bernard Green (private communication) has described this behavior on the part of the teacher as 'analogous' to the standard Christian doctrine of the Incarnation. (For a summary of that doctrine, see 5.3.1.) A similar 'analogy' was present in the action of the character in *'Heavens Above'* (5.3.2), who gave up the security of the routine of the established church, incurred overwhelming social opposition, and ended by taking another man's place in a spacecraft and becoming a block of ice in outer space. But these particular analogies fulfill four special conditions:

☐   One side of the analogy consists of physical, human acts.

☐   The other side of the analogy is the idea of redemption through Christ as the incarnation of God.

☐   The human acts are both motivated by and made possible by the actor's deep belief in the idea. They thus become, not just figurative *symbols* for the idea, and not just an analogy of it, but outward *signs* that the idea is active within the actor.

☐   The human purpose of the human acts is to help other humans to get something which they deeply desire and which is within the range of what humans actually can help one another to get: health, food, longer life, fluency in German, a feeling of self-respect, political freedom, and so on. It does not include such things as spiritual salvation or eternal life.

To the extent that an analogy meets all four of these conditions, it begins to take on some qualities of a *sacrament*, whether the human actions involved be a style of teaching, or of cooking, or of sharing a flat (Maley 1983). (My own view of life's activities, including teaching, is 'sacramental' in this special sense.)

5.4 Counseling-Learning: theory and practice

Let us return now from the theory to the practice of Counseling-Learning. Maley (1983) has expressed his belief that the 'humanistic' approaches are 'authoritarian' and 'not open to refutation' (p.80). He is by no means alone in this opinion. Perhaps, however, this warning is more appropriately directed, not against the approaches themselves, but against the movements that propagated them. No matter how arguable and potentially falsifiable the tenets, and even if they *can* be discussed with an attitude of 'readiness to be criticized and eagerness to criticize oneself' (Popper 1976, p.115), there still remains the question of whether the originators and proponents of the methods themselves show such an attitude.

As we shall try to show in 5.5, whatever the attitude of people in the Counseling-Learning 'movement' may have been, the approach itself is open to objective examination and evaluation. Myths and dogmas, no matter what their source, are indispensable precursors of theories (Popper 1976), and so they may be welcomed, attacked rationally, and then rejected, modified, or tentatively retained according to their content. But I believe the attitude of the originator and propagators of this method has been widely misunderstood by many who have only read about Counseling-Learning, or who have watched it only briefly. Such misunderstandings may have prevented people from profiting from its positive contributions to our understanding of the learning and teaching of languages.

Thus, some people have been offended by the requirement placed on trainees in Counseling-Learning, that they repeat back to the lecturer their understanding of what he or she has said without *expressing* any objections or reservations. This requirement is sometimes mistaken for a prohibition on the exercise of critical judgment. Its purposes, however, are quite different from that. They are (1) to help trainees to understand the intellectual content of what the speaker is saying, and (2) to help them develop the useful practical skill of understanding future communications from their students. After all, those communications, whether verbal or non-verbal, will to a large extent be about the students' world-2 objects (1.2.1) - their subjective experiences and impressions - and will not be confined to the hypotheses and theories of world 3. The purpose of the requirement was clearly not to stifle criticism, for each lecture session was followed by a period in which trainees were encouraged to bring up whatever intellectual objections or misgivings - and even personal feelings - the lecture has raised in them. Those reactions were met with the same careful understanding that the trainees had been asked to give to the lecture. In any case, Curran's writings contain no strictures against dissent.

It is true that, in my own observations of Curran, I never saw him at a time when he appeared willing to brook criticism or contrasting opinion. It may be that for him, serving as a maker of what Popper calls 'myth' was inconsistent with participating in the kind of systematic disputation described by Popper, and that he more or less deliberately chose the former role. It is also true, however, that I never saw the slightest indication that his staff felt that trainees should not criticize the system, or that teachers should not modify what they had learned before putting it into use. Their only concern was that the modified versions should not be publicly labeled as 'Counseling-Learning'; that theories and techniques which Curran did not agree with should not be represented as his.

In 1.4.2, I explained why I did not think it would be appropriate to dismiss Brumfit's or Brooks' maxims as mere 'acts of faith'. The same is true of Counseling-Learning. Reduced to its simplest form, it is based on a series of three statements:

☐ One can differentiate only what one has retained. (If one learns to make a differentiation and then forgets one or both of the items that were differentiated, the differentiation will be lost too.)
☐ The more of oneself one has put into something - physically, imaginatively, or both - the better one is likely to retain it.
☐ The more secure one feels in a learning situation, the more fully one is likely to put oneself into what one is studying.

There is no more difficulty in defining and measuring the terms of these three statements than in doing the same for the maxims of Brumfit and Brooks. In fact, the first and second combined are reminiscent of Brumfit's maxim.

Issues that critics have raised about Counseling-Learning include:

☐ Counseling-Learning fits Breen's (1987) description of a 'process syllabus', whose designer 'will not focus upon, select, subdivide or sequence content. ... A major priority of the designer is to provide a framework which enables teacher and learners to do these things themselves and [thus] create their own syllabus in the classroom in a creative and adaptive way' (p.166). But can such a free-form style of instruction fit into a large-scale program in which students must be able to transfer from one class or even from one school to another?
☐ How can the principles of Counseling-Learning be applied to large classes in conventional classrooms?
☐ If content is to be student-initiated, to what extent will it be possible to bring in language and content authentic to the culture of the target language?

☐ How many teachers are prepared to accept the kind of discipline required of a knower-counselor?

☐ How many students are willing to learn without being actively 'taught'?

☐ For how many students is the kind of security offered in a Counseling-Learning class necessary? For how many is it a positive annoyance?

The first three of these issues are practical, and are susceptible of practical answers. The others are more fundamental, calling into question the theoretical bases of Counseling-Learning.

5.5 Counseling-Learning and the humanisms

Of the five components of 'humanism' listed in 2.2.2, concern for personal feelings (H1), and for social relations (H2), are the most conspicuous in Counseling-Learning. Indeed, the language teaching application of Curran's ideas is called Community Language Learning. There is also considerable emphasis on responsibility (H3) and on self-actualization (H5). The humanistic concern for realization of intellectual potential (H4) seems to be subordinate to the rest. As for Auden's pair of 'anti-types' (2.4), Curran's handful of simple techniques (and I admire all of them) remind me of the Arcadian's 'saddle-tank locomotives' and 'overshot waterwheels'. His lack of evident interest in what was going on in the mainstream of language teaching reminded me that the Arcadian had no regular source of news from the outside world.

Aside from the categories mentioned above, the qualities required of the knower-counselor are largely those that have been traditionally thought of as feminine: accepting what the learner-client has originated and giving it back lovingly, in enhanced form; supporting the ego of the vulnerable protagonist; nursing and nurturing.

This chapter has provided the most explicit vindication possible for Maley's thesis that thinking about 'humanistic' teaching often contains a strong religious element. In 5.2 we looked at education, therapy, and other parts of life, and at Curran's insistence that they are continuous with one another. Although we have tried to show that Oller's misgivings about Curran's use of certain religious terms were attributable either to misinformation or to misinterpretation, it still true that Counseling-Learning as described in 5.2 is not inconsistent with a secular brand of humanism. Then in 5.3 we went on to explore the relationship between the sacred and the secular, and have considered the possibility that while there is discontinuity between the two, they are still inevitably and intimately tied to each other (5.3.6). This is itself an article of faith - one that is essentially 'religious' in the usual sense of that term. In Chapters 6 and 7 we will meet quite different articles of faith, beginning with a system (Gattegno's Science of Education) that is resolutely and consistently non-religious.

6 A second 'humanistic' educator: Caleb Gattegno

6.1 Introduction

Caleb Gattegno was a thinker and practitioner who made highly original contributions, first to the teaching of mathematics, and more recently to the teaching of languages and to education in general. His Silent Way is an approach that has frequently been labeled 'humanistic'. The largest part of this chapter will be devoted to summarizing his basic ideas. Readers who are interested in technical details of his method will find them in Gattegno's books for language teachers (1972, 1976a, 1985a). We will, however, begin this chapter with a brief look at the Silent Way in action.

6.1.1 Two vignettes

Don and Donna are teachers who work with beginning students in the same program. The equipment available to them includes:

☐ a chart on which the spellings for the individual sounds of the students' native language are displayed in color against a black background. All spellings for a given sound are grouped together, and have the same distinctive color. For example, in such a chart for English, *e*, *ey*, *ay*, and *eigh* would appear in the same list, with the same color, because of words like 'cafe', 'they', 'day', and 'sleigh'. The items *e* and *ai* would appear in a different list, with a different color, on account of words like 'set' and 'said'. Such a chart is called a *fidel*, from the Amharic word for 'alphabet'.

☐ a similar fidel for the spellings of the sounds in the target language. As far as possible, the same colors are used on both fidels for sounds which are the same, or nearly the same, in the two languages.

☐ a collapsible pointer.

Don's and Donna's goal is to familiarize their students with the sounds of the new language, and with some of the ways in which they are written.

Don's class

a. Don does not use the native-language fidel. 'After all', he reasons, 'my students already know how to read and spell in their native language. Why take time with that?' Instead, he hangs up the target-language fidel.

b. 'Today', he announces, 'we are going to learn to pronounce and read some sounds in your new language.'

c. Instructing the class to 'Listen carefully, and repeat after me', Don points to one of the items on the fidel, pronounces it, and the students repeat it in chorus.

d. After two or three choral repetitions, Don calls on individual students to repeat after him.

e. When a student's mimicry is correct, he says 'Good!' or gives some other form of overt encouragement.

f. When a student's response is incorrect, Don gives the student another chance. If a student has persistent trouble, Don tells the student what to do with his or her mouth (for example 'Round your lips and push your tongue forward'), or even draws a diagram.

g. After teaching several sounds and their spellings in this way, Don goes to the chalkboard, writes various syllables that consist of familiar vowels and consonants, and calls on the students to pronounce them first chorally and then individually. Don reacts to correctness and incorrectness as he did in (d.) and (e.).

h. Finally, he tests the students' progress by pointing to various written items or combinations of items, and calling on individual students by name to pronounce them.

i. By the end of the session, the students control much of the linguistic material that has been presented. In addition, Don's competent, efficient manner has given his students increased confidence that in this course they will be well taught.

Donna's class

a. Donna first hangs up the fidel for the students' native language. As she does so, she acts a little playful, but she says nothing. She looks less like a teacher than like a person who is inviting the students to join her in an enjoyable secret game.

b. She picks up the pointer, pauses dramatically, then points to one of the items on the fidel and by gesture asks 'How do you pronounce this?'

c. Since the students do not yet know for sure what they are supposed to do, they may hesitate. Donna waits. Or they may come up with responses that do not fit the item on the fidel. Again Donna waits.

d. When a volunteer gives an appropriate response, Donna gives no overt indication that the response was the desired one. She simply points to another item on the fidel and repeats the process.

e. During this phase, some students are replying aloud, often more or less in unison. Others are just watching and listening.

f. Donna gives the pointer to a student, and gestures for him or her to do what she herself has been doing.

g. The designated student goes to the fidel and points at items. Other students respond.

h. Donna monitors this phase carefully. If a response is consistent with what has been pointed to on the fidel, she remains outside the activity. If it is inconsistent, she gestures the message 'More work is needed here. Try again.'

i. Donna takes the pointer and has the students do all the spellings for a given sound (all the spellings that are colored alike and adjacent to one another on the fidel), one after the other. She treats several groups of items in this way.

j. Then Donna begins pointing to combinations of consonants and vowels. In this way, she leads the students to produce a few simple syllables.

k. Again with a mysterious flourish, Donna hangs the target-language fidel alongside the one the students have become familiar with, and repeats the above steps.

l. She begins with sounds that are identical or very similar in both languages. If students do not at first realize that the colors are a guide to pronunciation, she points from, for example, the white or red list on the native language fidel to something in the room, the name of which includes a 'white' or 'red' sound, and has students pronounce from it. Then she goes back to the new fidel.

m.   Where there are small differences between a target-language sound and the nearest sound in the students' native language, Donna puts this information across either (a) by gesture, or (b) by letting students guess how the sound is made and indicating which guess is right, or (c) as a last resort, by saying the sound once. This third expedient is the only time in the entire procedure that Donna has said anything.

n. By the end of the session, students have not only learned some of the linguistic material that has been presented, but they have also learned something about their own powers as learners.

6.1.2 Discussion of the vignettes

Donna is a Silent Way teacher, Don is not. What we have just seen Donna do is not necessarily the best technique for introducing the fidels. What Don did is not necessarily the most effective manner of presenting this material outside of the Silent Way, either. We have only described a pair of techniques that use the same equipment, for the same linguistic goals, with the same kind of class. From the differences between these techniques, we will be able to illustrate some of the principles of Gattegno's approach to education.

Both Don and Donna want their students to leave the lesson with *new inner resources* for using the target language. These resources will enable them to pronounce some of the sounds of the language, and to associate those sounds with their written representations. All of their students have brought with them certain *pre-existing resources*:

1   They can produce the sounds of their native language.
2   They can associate the spellings of their native language with its sounds.
3   Since babyhood, they have known how to take what comes into their ears, devise a way to make their speech apparatus approximate it, and then check their own production against what they hear and against the reactions of other people.

They also have certain *private resources* that change from moment to moment. Among those resources are:

4   They know what they have noticed, and what they are still unsure about.

5 They know whether they are ready to run risks, or whether they still prefer to listen and think without speaking.

During the lesson, students may or may not notice certain things. Some of these things are of a linguistic nature:

6 That the first fidel is for their native language.
7 That colors stand for sounds, forming a sort of non-written phonemic transcription.
8 That sounds are separable from spellings.
9 That there is no one-to-one correspondence between sounds and spellings.
10 That some of the resources they have brought from their native language can be transferred to use in the target language.
11 What they have to do with their speech apparatus in order to produce sounds of the target language.

Of the things to be noticed, others are of a more general nature:

12 It is possible to piece together a new linguistic resource one bit at a time.
13 Trial and error is an acceptable and efficient way to learn.
14 Abstract instructions (for example 'Pull your tongue farther back in your mouth') are not necessary; it is possible to form a direct link between what one hears and what one does with one's speech apparatus.
15 The teacher sees the student as someone trying to learn - trying to develop some new inner resources that he or she needs. She does not see the student as someone who is seeking rewards by pleasing her. She only provides the challenges and the feedback. The feedback, whether positive or negative, is the reward.
16 The student is the one who chooses how to use his or her speech muscles, and the student is the one who lives with the results.

Still more generally, students may notice:

17 That noticing things can be useful.
18 That to some extent, they are able to control how much and what they notice.

When learners draw on their own inner resources rather than borrowing from someone else, Gattegno says they are being *independent* (6.5.4). When he decided not to begin with the fidel in his students' native language (a.), Don was neglecting a great store of resources that they had already within them.

To the extent that learners choose among the resources available to them for a particular purpose, they are exercising *autonomy* (6.5.4). When Don had his students repeat after him (c.), he was permitting them to use their existing mechanical ability to parrot sounds without noticing how the sounds are made. In the preceding paragraph we saw that use of this mechanism allowed the students to ignore their independent resources. But it also deprived them of an opportunity to choose among those resources. When Donna did not tell her students what they were to do or how they were to do it (c.), she was requiring them to explore and to select from resources of at least two kinds. One was, of course, linguistic. The other had to do with possible activities and kinds of relationships.

In whatever ways they are required to check their productions against the reactions of the outside world, and must then 'stand by what they do', learners are being *responsible* (6.5.4). So, for example, Donna let her students know when and where more work was needed (h.).

Treating the lesson as a game helps the students to get away from the conventions of academic study, and to *reawaken the powers that all babies have*. Donna did this with her playfulness (a.) and mysterious flourishes (k.). Don, on the other hand, through his announcement of an academic goal (b.), immediately established the traditional teacher-student relationship.

When the teacher arranges matters so as to make it necessary for students to notice something that they might otherwise have overlooked, she is said to be *'forcing awareness'* (6.2.3). In step (i.), Donna forced her students to notice a new purpose for which color can be used.

By working as much as possible with the students' inner resources, and by encouraging independence, autonomy, and responsibility, the teacher is *subordinating teaching to learning*. Donna exemplified this principle by her careful monitoring of her students' work and of its results, by remaining outside the activity as much as possible and, incidentally, by her silence (h.). Don's overt corrections or confirmations of his students' output (e., f.) were extrinsic to the relationship between minds and challenges.

The words in italics summarize six key features of the Silent Way, each of which was more present in Donna's teaching than in Don's. In the remainder of this chapter, we will see how these features fit into Gattegno's ideas about education and about life.

6.1.3 The format of this chapter

Chapters 3 to 6 of *Teaching Languages: A Way and Ways* (1980) summarized what I then knew of Caleb Gattegno's Silent Way and the thinking behind it. Gattegno apparently considered that formulation to have been accurate as far as it went. But I have read much more of Gattegno since that time, and in any case, my focus then was on 'ways' of teaching rather than on 'humanism'. The present chapter may therefore serve to supplement Chapters 3 and 4 of *A Way and Ways*. But the title of this present chapter says nothing about 'the Silent Way'. The omission is deliberate. That often-cited, seldom-practiced, strikingly unconventional approach to language teaching is actually an instance of what Gattegno calls 'the Science of Education', which has captured the interest of many teachers of mathematics, reading, and foreign languages around the world.

According to the Popperian principles outlined in Chapter 1, the first step towards assessing a writer's contribution to theories of education should be to examine the 'world-3 objects' he or she has created: both his or her verbal statements and the ideas for which those statements stand. In Gattegno's case that step is particularly difficult, for four reasons: (1) many of his writings appeared only as 'restricted printings', unavailable through commercial publishers, and many of those are now out of print; (2) his ideas are those of a maverick - an original, a loner who read widely but seldom commented directly on the work of his contemporaries; (3) many of the terms he used are found in the writings of no one else, and (4) his prose style, though linguistically correct, is idiosyncratic.

For these reasons, any attempt by this writer, or any other, to reword and summarize Gattegno's thinking is almost certain to produce serious distortions. Sections 6.2 to 6.5 of this chapter are condensed from a summary that was checked with Dr Gattegno and with a number of other people familiar with his work, but even the most careful condensation may introduce new distortions. With that caveat in mind, let us proceed.

6.2 Basic concepts

To me, Gattegno's writings about his Science of Education read very much like a drama. The protagonist is a 'self'. Each of us is, in fact, a self plus whatever that self has created. The principal motivation for the action of the drama is a quest for freedom - freedom from the instincts and from the habitual behaviors that characterize what Gattegno calls 'pre-humans' (a term that includes most of us). When this freedom has been attained, but only then, the self can become fully Human-with-a-capital-H. Sections 6.2.1 to 6.4.4 will be, in effect, an account of that drama.

6.2.1 Energy and time

Although Gattegno's thinking goes far beyond the traditional physical sciences, he bases his entire system on two concepts that are essential to them: energy and time. In his words: 'Essentially energy and time are *at the origin of all realities*' (1985a, p.41) [emphasis added]. But Einstein, according to his famous formula $e = mc^2$ (energy equals mass times the velocity of light squared), showed that matter and energy are convertible into each other. Therefore the word 'energy' in this statement of Gattegno's is understood to include matter.

6.2.2 The four realms

For Gattegno, what the rest of us call 'the human race' exists simultaneously in four different 'realms'. In the first, we consist of nothing but atoms and molecules. In the second realm, we are made up of cells and tissues: configurations of atoms and molecules capable of metabolism. This, of course, sets us apart from non-living matter. In the third realm, we are members of a species - a configuration of tissues which has its own characteristic instincts and behaviors. In the fourth and final realm, Gattegno says 'it is permitted to each individual to transcend the species by getting rid of all instincts' (1979, p.12). This fourth realm is the realm of 'awareness', which is the quality that can make us truly human. Its most important function is to allow us to free ourselves from the limitations imposed in the first three realms. This fourth realm is therefore the realm of supreme importance.

6.2.3 Awareness, and awareness of awareness

One reason for the central place of awareness in Gattegno's scheme is that, as he says repeatedly, it is the only thing in us that is educable. He sometimes uses this term in the superficial sense in which we say 'I am aware of a change in the weather'. But he also uses it on a series of increasingly profound levels. He says that we may reach 'first awareness*es*, then awareness, and then awareness of our awareness, and then [a kind of awareness] that allows us to discover [awareness] in others' (1987, p.107) [emphasis added]. He also differentiates between a fleeting awareness of awareness and 'the permanent awareness of the awareness' (1977b, p.79). ('Awareness' is not identical with 'consciousness', which will be discussed in 6.3.2.) Gattegno goes so far as to say that '[This] awareness that only awareness is educable in man is ... showing that all other approaches to education [apart from Gattegno's] either are ineffective or are reducible to an education of awareness albeit in disguise' (1987, p.123).

6.2.4 The self as energy

Gattegno lists a number of attributes of the self: 'will', 'intelligence', 'patience', 'sensitivities', 'vulnerability', 'perception', 'retention', 'discrimination', 'abstraction', 'persistence', 'commitment' (1985a, p.4ff.), and, of course, 'awareness'. But if energy and time are at the origin of all realities, then the self must consist ultimately of energy. Gattegno is emphatic that the energy of the self has not only a *quantity* (what he calls a 'quantum') so small that it cannot be measured by any laboratory equipment. It also has a special *quality*. This quality enables the self to be aware of all kinds of energy, including itself. No individual's quantum is exactly like the quantum of any other individual. 'I am an *energy* system endowed with awareness. Hence I can become aware of the *energy* inputs I receive and know them for what they are' (1985a, p.44) [emphasis added].

6.2.5 Evolution

Fully developed awareness, and nothing else, can prove to be 'a *leap* that can generate the next layer of *evolution* for man' (1977b, p.79) [emphasis added]. In the lower three realms (6.2.2), Gattegno's meaning for 'evolution' is not unlike the standard Darwinian view: that new combinations or variations which arise by chance are retained and multiplied if they are suitable for the circumstances in which they arise, but if they are not suitable, they are lost. He says that some evolution is 'horizontal': in this type the possibilities and the implications of an innovation are explored and developed. But there is also 'vertical' evolution, which happens when a new principle or a new way of handling energy is introduced (1977b, p.70). Any 'horizontal' evolution is 'the unfolding of one possibility'. When the implications of that possibility have been found, an impasse is reached and a new vertical leap is needed if evolution is to continue (1977b, p.71). As examples of such leaps, Gattegno cites the advent of living cells in a world of non-living chemical compounds, or the advent of animals in a world which previously contained no non-vegetable life. (1977b, p.71ff.) Similarly, in the fourth realm, a new awareness may be a vertical leap that provides the basis for a new civilization.

In the long sweep of cosmic history, Gattegno discerns one overall principle, which is that 'our collective evolution has taken the turn of doing more and more with less and less' (1978, p.29). In the fourth realm, this 'doing more with less' is possible only through constant growth both in awareness and, as we said in 6.2.3, in awareness of awareness. Awareness of awareness brings the human race to the threshold of a major discontinuity: 'Two thousand six hundred years [after Socrates] the West is [still] in a similar situation needing to make the *leap* represented by that new awareness and seeing only its traditions as salvation' (1977b, p.73) [emphasis added]. In Gattegno's opinion, the West was mistaken in that view. He believes, in fact, that '*Today we are witnessing one more of those* [vertical] *leaps*' (1977b, p.70) [emphasis added]. That leap, if the race can make it, will lead to the dawn of a new age, in which '*Men* will begin *an adventure sui generis*' (1977b, p.72) [emphasis added].

This adventure is not open to all people, however, at least not in their present state. Gattegno distinguishes between 'pre-humans' and 'humans' (6.2). A 'man', as that word is used in the preceding quotation, means a fully human being, one who is '[an] evolved person who has reached consciousness and lived at a level of awareness that makes life transparent' (1988a, p.150). Evolution to full humanity is possible for each self individually, and also for the race as a whole. But it is a long process, requiring much sensitivity, much patience, much education of awareness. There is much more to it than can be accomplished even in an entire lifetime devoted to the enterprise.

6.2.6 Reincarnation

Therefore, says Gattegno, 'I have need of more lives *to chisel myself,* my quantum, further and [to] make me more myself by making me more human' (1978, p.52) [emphasis added]. It is the self's 'unique quantum of energy' that carries from one life to another the educated awareness of the evolving human being (1978, p.61). At conception, as Gattegno describes the process, a quantum 'descends' into a fertilized ovum, not to provide energy, but to direct the use of the energy that it finds there, including the energy contained in the DNA and in the mother's blood stream. As the weeks and months go by, the self uses its energy and its awareness in order to build for itself a *soma* - a body - and to cause that soma to operate in certain ways (1988a, p.7). In this process, the material of the soma becomes what Gattegno calls 'locked up' energy. This apparently does not mean that energy has become matter according to Einstein's formula. It means only that the way in which the matter in the body has been organized has resulted from application of energy that was controlled by the self and its agents. The soma *is* the self in the atomic and molecular realm (1987, p.85) (6.2.2). This process of 'objectivation' or 'locking up' of energy includes the formation of organs and tissues, but it also includes the minute changes that take place at the synapses of the central nervous system.

Death, then, is the mirror image of conception. The unique quantum of energy that is the self leaves the body and all of the organized systems that make up the body (1978, p.30), and rejoins the cosmos (1978, p.20). After the end of one life, the quantum chooses its mother and father for the next life 'so as to give [it]self the environment which will contribute to [its] continuing evolution in the human universe which has been created collectively in a world of individuals' (1978, p.48).

6.3 The self and its creatures

Sections 6.2.1 to 6.2.6 have sketched what Gattegno had to say about the nature and purpose of existence - his ontology and his teleology. In the pages that follow we will look at his understanding of how the self works, and from there we will move on to his theory of knowledge and learning, which in turn forms the basis for his ethics.

6.3.1 The self and energy

The self is 'free' energy (1978, p.9; 1988a, p.7), but because it is so small (6.2.4), it is able to deal with only one 'pinpointed' task at a time. Even for these tasks, it is insufficient to serve as a real *source* of energy. Rather, it does two things. First, it 'dwell[s] in the psychosomatic system at the place of command' (1978, p.20), and through use of 'amplifying mechanisms' it 'trigger[s]' two kinds of energy: the 'locked up' energies represented by the soma (6.2.6), and a kind of 'residual energy' which Gattegno calls the 'psyche'. Compared with the small size of the self, these energies are virtually inexhaustible. Second, through use of another kind of 'residual energy' called 'affectivity', the free energy of the self 'energize[s] the encounters with [that which] comes ([and which is] generally unknown) by concentrating on a pinpointed task representing this unknown' (ibid.). If we are to understand Gattegno's theory of learning, we must look further at these 'free', 'objectified', and 'residual' energies.

6.3.2 Consciousness

One of the distinctive features of Gattegno's model of education is that all of the work of the self is done 'consciously' (1973, p.6ff.). This applies even to the process of building the soma. But Gattegno's use of this word departs from common usage. In everyday language, to say that one is 'conscious' of something generally means that one is able to report on it in words. That Gattegno does not have this sense in mind is clear from his statement that consciousness is present everywhere in the soma: 'Consciousness ... is present in every cell and in every amount of energy in the soma' (1973, p.45), and that, as we saw in 6.2.6, it was present from conception. My best guess at this time is that by this term Gattegno means that consciousness is something like 'the ability to recognize or respond to recurrences of things, including itself', but that is only a guess. Gattegno is also quoted as having described 'consciousness' as 'energy which is deliberately mobilized' (de Córdoba, private communication), though that formulation of course leaves the word 'deliberately' undefined.

The rule of consciousness extends very far indeed, for the 'controls' referred to in 6.2.6 'are made from scratch with raw materials that have to be processed by two "knowing" delegates of consciousness, called "the psyche" and "affectivity", which remain to monitor once the task is deemed correctly completed' (1973, p.15). In 6.3.3 and 6.3.4 we will learn something about those 'delegates'.

6.3.3 The psyche

We have seen that, according to Gattegno, the self works consciously in all that it does from conception to death (6.2.6), and that it works only on one 'pinpointed' task at a time (6.3.1). Yet the simultaneous functionings of an individual in all four realms are exceedingly numerous and complex, and require constant supervision. Therefore the self as free energy must find a way 'to leave behind [some of the energies it has been able to direct] in a form we called "residual" to activate and dynamize the locked up soma'. This residual energy Gattegno calls the 'psyche', a 'substitute of the self remaining behind so as to free the self to take care of the next demand made on it ...' (1987, p.184).

The psyche performs an essential liaison function. It is in close contact with the locked up somatic energies, and so the self can delegate to it the tasks of survey, supervision, and maintenance of the functionings the self allotted to the structures. Hence the psyche too must have structures. This means that as the soma grows and gets objectified, so the psyche grows and gains new content. The psyche, which has been evolving continuously both *in utero* and afterwards, is therefore an integral part of memory (1987, p.199).

The brain, by contrast, is only one more part of the soma. As Gattegno puts it:

> the psyche is the part that knows and the brain the part that does. ... The self is the one which can know that it knows and [can] command the psyche to command the brain to command other organs or tissues ... (1987, p.201)

There is thus a kind of 'chain of command' (1977b, p.85; 1978, p.29) from the self to the psyche to the brain to other parts of the soma.

As I read Gattegno, the psyche is something like an adjutant or an executive officer or a regent in relation to the self. The psyche can direct almost all that a human being can do. It differs from the self, however, in that it has no will, and in that its creativity is limited (1987, p.201).

Because its domain is entirely limited to what has accumulated from past experience, the psyche is essentially a conservative force in personal functioning. Like a tradition-bound adjutant, it may 'get carried away with itself' and act in an 'insubordinate' manner, or, like a regent, it may try to become a usurper. [The material in quotation marks here is mine, not Gattegno's. EWS] The psyche may even deceive the self temporarily (1988a, p.11). But as soon as it has reason to question the way it has delegated its powers and has found a need to intervene, the self can 'call in affectivity and *intelligence* to transform the energy content of psychic movements and to return [itself] to its rightful place at the helm' (1988a, p.12) [emphasis added].

6.3.4 Affectivity
The second kind of residual energy is 'affectivity'. This concept is crucial to Gattegno's description of learning. Unfortunately, however, his discussion of it presents difficulties even for the sympathetic reader.

What Gattegno says is that, because both the psyche and affectivity are creations of the self, and because both are energy, 'residual energy can move from the psyche to affectivity, from entertaining the past to entertaining the future' (1988a, p.142). Like the psyche, 'affectivity is not free energy, but energy that the self keeps in contact with what it has already objectified [i.e. built into the physical body, including the synapses of the central nervous system (6.2.6)]. Although, in contrast to the psyche, affectivity operates at the service of the immediate future, it can mobilize the psyche to make it contribute all [that] it [the psyche, EWS] commands in the soma and in the mind' (1977a, p.5). Because affectivity is in contact with the objectified in the soma, it can do the same work as the psyche, but it operates only momentarily to force open a psychic gate or to reorganize energy within the objectified (1988a, p.14). The indispensable feature of affectivity is that it is not 'mortgaged to the past', and does not work through memory. It is therefore free to '*let the self entertain the new*' (1988a, p.142).

My guess is that if one were to rephrase the preceding paragraph in less specialized terminology, one might say, 'It is possible to use energy, not only to draw on the past, but also to focus on what lies at hand in the immediate future. Energy deployed in this way draws on all that has been learned earlier, but it may also use that information in creative ways which allow the learner to escape the patterns of the past.' But this is only a guess.

6.3.5 Intelligence

Two other elements, mentioned in some of the above quotations, that play important roles in the work of the self are intelligence and the will. As Gattegno uses the word 'intelligence', it is

> the movement of the self mobilizing energy, [mobilizing that part of the past not actually called in in the meeting of a challenge]. It can be psychic intelligence that would still keep things as they were, or affective intelligence that would make possible the introduction of a change. Both intelligences are seen by the self as mobilizers of past capabilities ... (1988a, p.12) [bracketed portion is from the 1975 edition]

Stated in another way:

> intelligence is that aspect of the self which ... recognizes that the instruments called upon are adequate to the task, or if they are not, mobilizes other available parts of the psyche or the self which did not emerge of themselves. (1987, p.155)

Intelligence is only an aspect of the self, and is not itself energy, so it can be effective only with the help of affectivity, which is energy (1987, p.158).

Again, one may hazard a paraphrase in more ordinary language: 'Intelligence consists in: (1) recognizing the demands of the task at hand; (2) recognizing which elements of existing relatively specific knowledge and skills are appropriate for meeting those demands, and (3), where existing specific knowledge and skills are inadequate, recognizing which more general knowledge and skills might contribute toward dealing effectively with the task.' Once more, however, this is only my guess.

6.3.6 The will

But intelligence alone is not what sets man apart from the rest of the animal kingdom. It is intelligence and will working together that will be '*the next domain of evolution* trying to produce the new' (1977b, p.36) [emphasis added]. Just as instincts are characteristic of the third realm (6.2.2), so the will is the hallmark of the fourth realm, for it is 'capable of *holding down instinctual reactions and of letting the individual explore* what is unkown, and even threatening' (1977b, p.35) [emphasis added]. And of course, what mobilizes the will is awareness, including awareness of the will (1976a, p.8; 1977b, p.50).

6.3.7 The bag

We come now to the last item in our inventory. Gattegno's theory of learning consists largely of an analysis and delineation of the interaction of the seven elements we have just met: the *self* as free energy, with its attributes of *awareness*, *will,* and *intelligence*; the *psyche* and *affectivity* as residual energy, and the *soma* as objectified energy.

Before going on to look at that theory, however, we must mention the 'bag'. As Gattegno describes it:

> Wherever we go we carry ourselves and ... what we move about is 'contained in a bag', of which our skin is a token. All items studied by anatomists, physiologists, neurologists, embryologists, etc., are in our bag. ... But ... we must also place in our bag our perceptions, our habits, our thoughts, for they too, can be transported like our bones, muscles, and organs, wherever we go. Our religious views, our tastes are in our bag as are our sentiments, feelings, resolutions, etc. (1973 p.4ff.).

The 'bag' is a concept to which Gattegno gives relatively little space, and he does not say much about the connections between it and the seven elements listed above. It is mentioned here because the metaphor fits so well into his description of knowing, learning, and teaching.

6.4 Knowing and learning

6.4.1 Ignorance

Gattegno's view of knowing and learning is derived from his concept of ignorance. For Gattegno, ignorance is not bad, it is not threatening, and it is not something to be overcome. It stands simply for the fact that outside the 'bag' there is an endless and unpredictable range of possible stimuli - 'energy impacts' - that will from time to time impinge on the 'bag' (1987, p.54). No amount of knowledge can reduce our ignorance, and ignorance has little to do with our knowledge (1988a, p.200).

6.4.2 Life and education

For Gattegno, education is virtually synonymous with true living, so that what he labels his 'Science of Education' is in effect a fully developed philosophy of life. The essence of education, like the essence of living, lies in meeting 'the unknown' in all its mystery and majesty - 'To know is the aim of life ...' (1987, p.59) - even though no amount of knowing can ever reduce ignorance. Superficially, this sounds like an echo from Popper (1.2.2). As we have already seen, however, Gattegno is referring here not to factual or propositional knowledge, but to something more like awareness. The meaning of living thus becomes *meeting what comes* (1978, p.60) [emphasis added], by which I think he means dealing with the successive challenges of what comes to one out of the inexhaustible reservoir of the unknown. The quality of one's life depends on the quality of one's responses to 'what comes'. Hence Gattegno's emphasis on affectivity (6.3.4) and will (6.3.6).

Elsewhere, Gattegno defines 'learning' in almost the same words, as 'meet[ing] the descending unknown' (1985a, p.5); it is 'equivalent to living, to [exchanging] *our time (which is our wealth) for experience ...*' (1985a, p.10) [emphasis in original]. Just how this exchange is made constitutes a major issue in Gattegno's theory of education. But it cannot be made at all if one is 'being lived by one's past' (1988a, p.viii).

Learning, of whatever kind, takes place in a series of four phases. First, the self finds itself facing an 'unknown' - a new 'impact' from outside its 'bag'. *Phase one* is made up of these contacts with the unknown (1985a, p.3ff.). Next, the self 'hesitates and uses time to try to make sense of' the new impact. Presumably during this time the self is consulting the information represented by the locked up configurations of energy that it has put together as the result of experience (6.3.1). *Phase two* lasts so long as the self is analyzing, questioning, trying. Eventually, the self recognizes either some of its attributes or some its own reactions to the unknown impact. This is the beginning of *Phase three*, which ends with mastery, when the new material is available for a new encounter with a new unknown. This introduces the *Fourth phase*, which closes the previous cycle and prepares for the next learning (ibid.).

6.4.3 Criteria

Learning, then, takes place when the self meets challenges that come with new impacts from the unknown. These new impacts 'force new awarenesses' (a phrase that appears several times in Gattegno's writings). The results of the new learning, whether facts or awarenesses, are 'objectified' (6.2.6) in the brain. The direct outcome of objectified awarenesses are what Gattegno calls 'criteria'. A standard (a 'criterion') is suitable for adoption - subject, of course, to revision in the light of later experiences - just as soon as it seems to give the desired results in dealing with the world (1985a, p.24). A major cause of mistakes in day-to-day living [and speaking!] is lack of the appropriate inner criteria (1976b, p.27). A good teacher, then, whether of language or of anything else, is one who *'force[s] awareness and thus generate[s] criteria ...'* (1985a, p.66) [emphasis added]. Criteria are formed largely through the use of intuition - through confirming or disconfirming guesses by a process of trial and error (1985a, p.23). Indeed, intuition is in general 'the most important way of knowing' (1987, p.80), and trial and error is valued as a way of learning.

Gattegno distinguishes *inner* criteria from *intellectual* criteria: the latter are useful only for certain people and under certain circumstances (1985a, p.22). Perhaps this distinction is related to that between using language on the basis of unverbalized 'regularities', and using language with the application of explicitly formulated 'rules' (Stevick 1989, p.92). Inner criteria can also be distinguished from *external* criteria, to which they are superior. Inner criteria are derived from observation of one's own experience with impacts from the unknown. External criteria are formed 'with only one outside criterion in mind: *approval from others*. ... To free [itself] from *this calamitous situation*, the self, with the help of wiser selves if they are available', must starve out any such expectations derived from the psyche, generating in their place a set of inner criteria based on *'feedback from reality rather than from people'* (1988a, p.49ff.) [emphasis added].

6.4.4 Ogdens

We have said that a 'criterion' is something which provides a basis for choosing among available alternative actions. Without criteria it would be impossible to act coherently or effectively. Some of the available actions among which we choose are ones that we have made up ourselves, either by internal experimentation or by combining parts from various other actions that we have already mastered. Other actions, however, are ones that have been invented by others, and are from our point of view completely arbitrary.

The example that Gattegno uses most frequently are the words of one's native language in contrast with those of a language learned later in life, but elsewhere (1985a, p.67) he refers in a similar way to the learning of inflectional affixes and various other formal features of a language. In talking about the building of this sort of criterion, Gattegno uses the term 'ogdens', named after the British scholar C.K. Ogden.

Gattegno sometimes describes ogdens as a 'process' (1988a, p.208), sometimes as a pedagogical outcome (1973, p.85), but sometimes (and I think this is closest to his intention) as 'energy':

> 'Ogden' is the name we have given to the [amount of] *mental energy* mobilized to retain an arbitrary sound or an arbitrary connection. One must pay as many ogdens as there are color rectangles on the Sound/ Color Chart ... (1985a, p.54) [emphasis added]

Although ogdens are to be 'paid', they are available in unlimited numbers (1985a, p.74). The result of the payment of ogdens - or the basis for saying whether or not they have actually been 'paid' - seems to be the dependable availability of the new formal unit (1976a, p.9). Elsewhere, however, the sufficiency of ogden-payment appears less clear: 'Retention [of new elements EWS] results both from the payment of ogdens *and* from practice' (1985a, p.74) [emphasis added]. The words 'both from' in this quotation might mean 'from either ... or from ...', or they might mean 'from a combination of ... and ...'. Gattegno's intention appears to be the latter. Elsewhere he says: 'Because awareness opens doors and practice produces facility we know that neither can be considered as sufficient on its own' (1987, p.124). Once these arbitrary units have been acquired in this way, they may recombined through the use of intelligence, which does not require any further 'payment of ogdens' (1985a, p.64).

The act of postulating a new unit and naming it after someone tends to highlight that unit for readers, and to expose it to criticism. This certainly has been true for the ogden. If indeed the ogden is intended to denote *some fixed quantity* of *energy*, then a question can be raised about its size. Gattegno however at no time (as far as I am able to find) ever actually *said* that all ogdens have to be of the same size. This omission may have been significant. To me at least, the most important aspects of the 'paying of ogdens' are not the *quantity* of energy or even the *use* of energy, but the facts that (1) energy is used *in a way that is different* from how it is used in ordinary contact with the world, and that (2) the paying of an ogden is a discrete act, readily locatable in time. It is an academic or quasi-academic act, an attempt to retain a word or a sentence or a verb ending or whatever *for its own sake on the basis of a single exposure*, rather than meeting it repeatedly as a part of ongoing experience. One is reminded of the much-discussed contrast between 'acquisition' and 'learning', or between informal and academic learning. But that is this writer's own reinterpretation of Gattegno. It is not supportable by any quotation from him.

6.5 How should we live?

6.5.1 Seek and accept uniqueness

Because he regarded himself as a scientist, Gattegno was not disposed to tell people what they 'should' or 'should not' do. Nevertheless, his work emphasizes certain principles from which readers are likely to extract norms. Thus we saw in the earlier sections of this chapter that for Gattegno the *goal* of existence, both individual and collective, is to move from pre-humanity to full humanity - to the status of Man-with-a-capital-M. The *protagonist* in this odyssey is a tiny quantum of energy that is qualitatively different from all other such quanta. The chief *means* by which this quantum can hope to achieve its goal is the education of its own awareness. Learning, then, is not just an isolable, optional part of life; it is the essence of all living. And learning - responding to the unknown - leads to what is *new* and to what makes the learner-responder *unique*:

> To be happy in any routine denies our humanity. (1988a, p.177)

> [The self should not allow itself to be] inhibited from doing what is *properly human, i.e., entering the future*. (1988a, p.15) [emphasis added]

> The fact that life in the fourth realm is human means precisely that the evolution of humans takes place at the level of *producing the new* and not in perpetuating the past, as in the non-human. (1978, p.50) [emphasis added]

> Men are free from asking but they do not cease to live. They will use their freed energy in *the exploration of the possibilities of human living and conscious living, its new form*. (1988a, p.157) [emphasis added]

> [Intuition is] the proper way of knowing of today, the most fruitful, the one that produces the blossoming of *new ways of looking at everything*. (1987, p.81) [emphasis added]

6.5.2 Adopt an attitude of relativism

This quest for uniqueness in one's responses to the uniqueness of the unknown means that the self must avoid what Gattegno calls 'absolutes', by which he seems to mean 'ideas that are thought to be valid for all people, at all times, under all circumstances'. He has written: 'In humanity, there are only persons, and *the only absolute* is that one cannot live outside one's awareness of oneself' (1987, p.110) [emphasis added]. A self that dedicates itself to one or another absolute will find its vision of reality blurred (1977e, p.81). But the tyranny of absolutes is now ended:

> The successive absolutes of the past centuries ... regarded us as beings originating elsewhere, created by a power foreign to ourselves, and explaining us from outside. We were spiritual insofar as the gods or God recognized us as belonging to them, we were rational insofar as we adopted a certain logic, we were free insofar as we subscribed to a certain political, economic or social creed. Outside these absolutes we were [outcasts, lost, etc.]. Idealism and science have concurred to liberate us from absolutes by revealing to us humanity in its entirety and inspired by the idea of evolution in accustoming us to *relativity*. (1962, p.9)

An attitude of relativism is necessary to the kind of evolution Gattegno is describing:

> A proper contact with oneself may result in a total relativity of our human universe, just as was required in the exact sciences where observations include the observers and where we want to understand what each of us meets as a response to the probes we place in the universe. Total relativity is a freeing movement because of its truth. *What it actually means is that from the place which is ours we look at our world in such ways that we see what can be revealed of that universe according to our instruments.* For each of us the world is what we can manage to let be revealed to us. (1988a, p.182) [emphasis added]

Necessary though they may be, the death of absolutes and the birth of the age of relativity represent a painful process which pre-humans are unwilling to undergo:

> Those who speak on behalf of mankind [as contrasted with humanity! EWS] [do not know the *relativity* of awareness and awareness of relativity, but only know] absolutes to which they *adhere* and from which they draw the justifications for their conviction that the actions they propose are right. ... The supporters of mankind could achieve their ends if they could shift to becoming holders of the *relativity that generates tolerance of the other*. But ... they do not seem ready to pay the price: abandonment of absolutes passed on from times when awareness was not the concern of people. (1987, p.110ff.) [emphasis added]

6.5.3 Love others

This tolerance for others leads to respect for others, and respect is the first prerequisite for love:

> To make people into what one believes they should be is clearly to satisfy oneself and not to leave them to be as much themselves as they can be. Hence love is not at work here. (1977 p.37)

> Love fertilizes one's imagination and places in oneself the presence of others as autonomous beings who are endowed with much one knows to be attributes of oneself - in particular, feelings, a will and a vision of the world. Through this love, by making oneself move to accept others, others accept oneself. The *respect* for their reality and all that they are engaged in is a form that love can take and a channel for its expression. (1973, p.121) [emphasis added]

6.5.4 Become more independent, autonomous and responsible, and encourage these qualities in others

One quality that the evolving self must develop is *independence*: 'Independence is the notion of our being aware that *we can only count on ourselves*' (1976, p.45) [emphasis added]. Independence therefore requires us to be fully aware of the resources that we have within ourselves. But we must be equally aware of our power to employ those resources in meeting challenges from the unknown: 'The basis of all *independence* is in the realization that what one does is accessible to and *can be acted upon by an alert self*, the same self that crosses roads and climbs steps' (1988a, p.214) [emphasis added].

A second quality is *autonomy*:

> The autonomy of speakers is the outcome of *the existence of choices* of expressions available to them. ... The facility of producing equivalent expressions restates again and again our autonomy in our use of our language. (1976a, p.49) [emphasis added]

> To be autonomous [is] to have *initiatives of our own* in areas where we have achieved our aims, i.e., to be able to produce what we want for the purpose we want. (1975, p.149) [emphasis added. This section was omitted from the 1988 edition.]

When one's choices (autonomy) in how to use one's inner resources (independence) lead to appropriate results, one has been *responsible*:

> There is a third component in our use of language, the one we call responsibility. Clearly we are first responsible because we have a will

and it is being used when we say something or refrain from saying anything. We are also responsible in what we do in preparing for the utterances. ... We are selective and therefore responsible for the selection. (1976a, p.49)

[Students] become responsible to the extent that they can systematically and carefully use what has been made available to them ... (1976a, p.16)

In this last quotation, Gattegno is referring to the information made available through the coloring of the charts, but the principle of course applies to information from all sorts of 'impacts'.

6.5.5 Seek greater freedom for yourself and for others

Uniqueness, relativism, respect, love, independence, autonomy, and responsibility all contribute toward freeing the self in its evolutionary quest for full humanity and 'more abundant life' (1973, p.7):

Elsewhere we have worked on other areas in which man is a learner, and every time our proposals have been designed to *free* students deliberately from dependence and aim at autonomous and responsible learners. By using what each student brings to the task and by being acquainted with how one learns what is implicit in skills and capabilities, we can help others become *freer* of inhibitions, of anxiety, of all the hampering moves and at the same time make them experience an expansion of their self in the new universe open to them. This kind of teaching belongs to the theme of this book. (1988a, p.223) [emphasis added]

6.5.6 Avoid adhering, believing, interfering, and imposing

All of the positive points in 6.5.1 to 6.5.5 carry with them a few negative implications. One should not adhere to standards derived from the past and preserved in the psyche:

[One] milestone [in re-education] consists in knowing that when we are engaged in vital activities there is *neither failure nor success, only successive moments*, each one teaching us something important in relation to the activity. (1988a, p.201)

Instead of remaining under the control of the psyche, Gattegno says, we should re-educate ourselves to the point where we can live

without expectation but not without drive,
without investment but not without commitment,
without ambition but not without resolution,
without egocentricity but not without presence ... (1988a, p.202)

In particular, one should not adhere to ideas or formulations derived from the past and from others rather than from one's own experience. Such adherence is what Gattegno apparently means by 'belief':

> To believe is to give reality to that which does not generate in the self the awareness that is akin to the awarenesses that the self produces when concerned only with itself, and for which it can say, 'I know.' *Knowing produces freedom, belief generates dependence.* (1973, p.117) [emphasis added]

In this sense, believing is incompatible with the self's evolution from pre-human to human status:

> Rebels of all kinds exist because man can hold beliefs; that is, he can accept as true what does not meet the criteria that accompany the functionings of the self. These positions can be rejected without violating one's sense of truth precisely because it was not involved in the first place; and so because of belief, there are rebels. (ibid.)

> Learning [unencumbered by adherences and beliefs EWS] will contribute to making each of us more of a person, more oneself and, because of this, *contribute to collective evolution.* (1988a, p.222) [emphasis added]

One should not obstruct the evolutionary quest either for oneself or for others: 'By undertaking to experiment with what presents itself ..., people evolve' (1977b, p.75). But 'by refusing to experiment with what comes ... some people *interfere with evolution*' (1977b, p.74) [emphasis added]. But if one should respect others and refuse to try to make them over into what one believes they should be (6.5.3), then some might ask how Gattegno himself can advocate a system of thought such as the one we have been examining in this chapter. The answer is that, although he takes a clear stand, he is equally clear that he is *offering* it to others rather than trying to *impose* it on them. This refrain is found over and over in his writings:

> The meaning of this essay can best be described by saying that it aims at making me understand my place in the universe better. In so doing, *others perhaps* will join me, retaining from their reading that indeed, for them too, that is the case. (1978, p.i) [emphasis added]

> Those leads yielded vistas that I [may] one day find [have] become major preoccupations for me *and perhaps for others.* (1977b, p.iii) [emphasis added]

> Do I want to be accepted through an idea I have of myself? Or just be myself and *see who will be moved to become a companion ...?* (1988a, p.172) [emphasis added]

It took me many many years to make sure that I neither fooled myself nor would fool the others. Now, I do not mind if nobody shares what I have found, and *this not minding has been integrated in my understanding of understanding* and stands firmly as an awareness ... (1978, p.65) [emphasis added]

6.6 Commentary

6.6.1 Gattegno's view of himself

This leads us finally to the place Gattegno sees for himself in the process of collective evolution. In general, he points out that 'Some of us leave contributions in [various] realms, such as our works of art, our tools, our books, our organizations, etc.' (1978, p.45).

Applying this to himself, he says that 'I definitely knew myself as insignificant with respect to the totality of the universe. However, ... I could ... gain some significance by making an original contribution to knowledge' (1979, p.6). His own original contribution is derived from his special gifts for self-observation and awareness: 'For the moment only a small number of men have succeeded ... [in acquiring] this knowledge of themselves as spiritual beings and as evolutionary energy ...' (1962, p.10). Like any other evolutionary innovation, this knowledge can spread to succeeding generations:

> These are collective facts of awareness which had first to be found in individual awarenesses and made available to those others who would pay the price of obtaining them for themselves, and then were given to all for nothing, as a matter of course, as a birthright. This descent of awareness into *one person*, and from him to others, and then to all, is another fact of awareness which is increasingly becoming collective every day. (1987, p.120) [emphasis added]

Gattegno appeared to view himself as such a person. Again:

> The renewal of mankind takes place when *someone* finds in himself and his life a way of handling energy that integrates - by transcending it - what was available [before this discovery was made]. This vertical evolution has been at work ... in the three realms of the cosmic, the vital, and the instinctual and many more times in the fourth realm of man. Today we are witnessing one more of these leaps. (1977b, p.70) [emphasis added]

At least in the science of education and at least today, Caleb Gattegno was such a 'someone'. He was first and foremost an educator, and:

The educator ... will not be discouraged by the traditional battles between the future which reaches out with its truth and the past which holds us back in the shape of organized bodies. He will make it known, loud and clear, that his experience assures him that he speaks of a sensible reality and that everyone can equally well assure himself of it. But if people refuse to follow him, *his* truth, which is *the* truth, will remain outside the awareness of those who refuse him credit and do not try in their turn to reach his level. All his actions will be based however on this truth ... (1962, p.11) [emphasis in original]

Gattegno commented a quarter of a century later: 'I cannot consider that anyone will follow me. Certainly not at my request' [private communication].

6.6.2 Other people's views of Gattegno

In 5.4 concern was expressed that negative reactions to the personalities involved in Counseling-Learning may have interfered with some people's ability to profit from the positive contributions of that approach. The same thing seems to have been true for Gattegno's approach to education. In this section I would like to place on record my own experiences in this area.

A number of people have said that Gattegno was 'overbearing', even 'arrogant'. There is no denying that his manner in public appearances was often consistent with that description. There are two possible explanations here. The first might be that Gattegno simply lacked skill in interpersonal relations. After all, he was by his own description an introspective man, Kipling's 'cat that walked by himself', unconcerned to please other people (private communication). Another guess is that Gattegno's sometimes-abrasive public behavior was simply an expedient to ensure that people were both emotionally and intellectually involved with what he was doing in their presence. This second hypothesis receives support from two observations. One is that I have never heard of rude behavior in his face-to-face encounters with individuals who are not challenging his ideas. The other is that, in print, though he did not respond directly to criticism, neither did he reject it:

I am, as a scientist, only concerned to speak about what I consider to be the truth in the matter. *My readers must judge me* mainly on whether I have departed from this imperative. (1985b, p.vi) [emphasis added]

While I believe that [my] new approach has much to commend it, and while I very much hope that it will be given as fair a trial as my previous suggestions to colleagues in schools, I must point out that it is a one-man proposal based on one man's experience, *of necessity limited*, and that the most important contribution of this work is the opening of new vistas in education that should excite a new generation of people *to investigate and to experiment with what they find behind the doors that are now put ajar*. (1972, p.xiv)

My personal experiences with Gattegno also support the second hypothesis. After reading the first draft of 6.1 to 6.6.1, Gattegno told me that, though my facts were essentially correct, he was disappointed that I had not provided my own '*creative reactions*' to his thought [private communication]. I also know firsthand (1985a, p.ii) that he was quite gracious about accepting unsolicited criticism on matters not part of the substance of what he had written.

Gattegno was emphatically unwilling to be thought of as a philosopher. He variously described himself as a 'scientist' and [private communication] as just 'a pedestrian technician', but one 'who is not bound by any a priori, and is ready to alter radically his thinking if some evidence requires it'. His aim was only 'to put into circulation how I am educated by my contact with the challenges I encounter'.

Here, then, is another myth-maker, but one who, as we have seen, explicitly invited criticism and testing. Quite possibly, on those occasions when he violated norms of polite society, he was simply continuing to exemplify, in ways that most people did not expect, the same teaching approach he was trying to convey to trainees: he was doing what he thought necessary in order to give his hearers a next minimal something-to-work-with - something that would enable them to move themselves one step nearer to the goal they had in coming to his sessions, which was to find out what he had to contribute to their professional and personal resources.

Users of the Silent Way have varied greatly in their manner of dealing with others in the profession. Certainly some have shown 'the expulsive power of a new affection', the zeal and intolerance that come naturally to those who are sure no one before them was right. But as with Counseling-Learning, we may hope that outsiders to this movement will not allow that to interfere either with practical or with intellectual investigation of the many potential values in Gattegno's work.

6.6.3 Rational discourse and Gattegno's Science of Education

The Silent Way is a practical application of the 'Science of Education'. It is, in effect, a claim that students learn more quickly, and retain better, if they are taught according to the following four steps:

☐   Before doing anything, the teacher forms a tentative mental image of what resources the student already has available.

☐   The teacher's activity is limited to giving the student some minimal new information or setting some small clearly-defined task that will enable the student to build the next appropriate resource for him or herself, and to providing impersonal feedback.

☐   The teacher allows plenty of time for the student to do whatever internal work is necessary to build that next resource.

☐   On the basis of the student's performance, the teacher updates his or her image of what the student has available, and repeats the above three steps.

Here again, as in 1.4.2, certain terms need to be specified. Expressions like 'resource', 'available', and 'minimal' need publicly usable descriptions, and to the extent that such descriptions can be provided, the claim is potentially testable. To the extent that it is not testable, it can still be examined for circularity, for internal consistency, and for its consistency with other 'not-yet-disconfirmed conjectures'. In this sense it can be investigated with the 'critical attitude' that Popper recommends (1.2.3) in dealing with world-3 objects for which direct falsification is not feasible.

Language teachers may question certain aspects of the Silent Way. Perhaps the most frequently raised objection is the difficulty of maintaining the silence and of using the charts, the rods, and the other equipment with large classes. There are two answers to this objection. From the practical point of view, a number of teachers have succeeded with the Silent Way in large classes around the world. And from the point of view of methodology, we must remember that neither the charts, nor the rods, nor even the silence, is essential to the method.

Another question that is frequently raised about the Silent Way is how students can be exposed to adequate samples of natural language if they are constantly given one small 'challenge' after another as they work with the limited materials that Gattegno has devised. A partial answer to the question is, again, that the essence of the methodology is found in the four points listed at the beginning of this section, and not in the specific technology through which the method has usually been demonstrated.

A more serious practical concern about the Silent Way is that it technically elegant, but also quite austere. It requires of the teacher an extraordinary degree of intellectual concentration and personal discipline. This fact necessarily limits the number of teachers who will find it compatible with their way of relating to their classes.

But the Silent Way is only one application of Gattegno's Science of Education. Several issues are likely to catch the attention of critical readers as they examine that body of thinking. Perhaps the most conspicuous is Gattegno's idea of reincarnation, and the central place which that concept occupies in his account of life and education (6.2.6). The evidence that he offers (1978, pp.39-44) in support of this idea is at best introspective and anecdotal. Few readers will be emotionally neutral here. Again, however, it is to be hoped that emotional reactions on this issue will neither block the careful examination of the rest of his work, nor lead to its uncritical acceptance.

A related issue is how a tiny 'quantum of energy' (6.2.4) can acquire and retain the wide range of 'awarenesses' accumulated through the experiences of a lifetime. Such 'energy' must be qualitatively different from all other kinds of energy. But if this is so, some will ask, why call it 'energy' at all? Is Gattegno simply assigning this name and description to an unknown cause of certain effects that he has observed - sketching a 'black box' (3.2.3) from which to draw arrows to the phenomena for which he wants to account? The idea of a small and unexhausted agent is reminiscent of Widdowson's description of 'capacity', which 'enables [a child] to ... acquire a competence in a particular language. ... This capacity is not used up by conversion into competence, but remains as an active force for continuing creativity' (1983, p.26).

A third issue is Gattegno's postulation of a large number of entities in communication with one another: 'the self', 'the will', 'the psyche', and so on (6.3.1 to 6.3.7). Are these again just metaphoric 'black boxes'? Or worse, are they a whole team of homunculi, serving to obscure rather than to elucidate human functioning?

Further issues arise out of the importance which Gattegno attaches to evolution and relativity. Have those ideas, as Gattegno believes, fundamentally altered the nature and the potential destiny of the human race, or have they not? To what extent can we in fact enter a 'new age' through application of our own intelligence and power? Another point, related to this question, is that if the unknown were merely a completely diverse, random jumble of not-yet-experienced impacts, then the formation of a criterion based on previous experience would be of no help at all in dealing with still later impacts from the unknown, and so there would be no point in forming criteria. Gattegno clearly does not intend this interpretation. But if the unknown is not a random jumble, why is it not? Where does its orderliness come from?

6.6.4 Gattegno's Science of Education and the humanisms

Finally, where does Gattegno's work stand in relation to the versions of humanism described in 2.2.2, 2.4, and 2.5? The answer depends on whether we are looking at practice, or at faith. In the *practice* of the leading exemplars of the Silent Way, students frequently have an experience of intense concentration, and of achieving, within a very short time, results that can only be described as amazing. Yet the demeanor of some Silent Way teachers is often quite crisp, even peremptory, and students sometimes feel themselves being guided in ways they do not understand, toward goals they have not yet glimpsed. McNeill (1982, p.119ff.) appears to have had this kind of experience. The kinds of 'awarenesses' on which the Silent Way typically concentrates are in the areas of linguistic form and cognitive functioning (ibid.). 'Independence' and 'autonomy' are largely confined to the same areas, and do not extend to selection of content or types of activity. Again, this writer's observations largely agree with McNeill's here. The Silent Way commonly produces strong positive - and sometimes strong negative - emotions in learners. Indeed, the education of awareness and the building of criteria with regard to affect is a goal of the whole approach. Nevertheless, affective matters receive very little overt attention from the teacher. Unlike Counseling-Learning (Chapter 5), the Silent Way de-emphasizes the learner's vulnerability. Instead, it emphasizes the learner's potential, including potential for dealing with negative affect.

Of the emphases within humanism listed in 2.2.2, the two which are most conspicuous in the Silent Way are on human intellectual potential (H4) and the shaping of the unique self (H5). The approach probably pays less attention to social relationships (H2) and individual feelings (H1) than some approaches that are not ordinarily called 'humanistic'. The net effect is reminiscent of the Utopian's attitude in Auden's poem (2.4). In contrast to Counseling-Learning (5.5), most Silent Way teachers this writer has observed or learned from illustrate traditionally masculine qualities, bringing to their students new 'challenges' or 'impacts' (6.4.2, 6.4.3) from outside, as a result of which they expect that some sort of desired new structure will take shape within the 'bag' (6.3.7) of each learner.

In many respects Gattegno's *faith* clearly fits with that of Kurtz and the secular humanists (2.2.1):

- ☐ He rejected the supernatural.
- ☐ He placed great value on science.
- ☐ He believed that human beings are able to transform themselves individually and collectively so as to enter a new age.

☐   He was unwilling either to follow or to establish any fixed tradition.

But as secular humanists go, Gattegno's emphasis on intuition (6.4.3), together with his unreadiness to engage either in controlled experimentation or in the kind of two-way critical discussion that Brumfit and Maley have asked for, make him something of an Arcadian.

Though he rejected traditional religions, Gattegno created what is almost a religion-surrogate. His writings provide their own epistemology, ontology, and teleology (that is, their own doctrines of knowing, and of the nature and goals of being). They also provide their own ethics, and even their own hopeful picture of what happens after death. In relation to this body of doctrine, the amazing results that Gattegno and others have attained with the Silent Way constitute a body of validating miracles (Stevick 1980, p.287). It is not surprising that his thinking holds great appeal for many people today. As one of his long-time students has put it:

> Dr. Gattegno [was] the only educator who constantly challenged me to be my best and then to become even better. His confidence in the learning powers he said we all possess was inspiring, and his ability to stimulate these powers in others was often uncanny.

My own position on Gattegno's humanism is like my position on the other forms of humanism in language education. Those of us who cannot fully accept the faith that underlies his Science of Education can still make profitable use of the Silent Way. We may also come to understand our own faiths better for having paid careful attention to his. And even if we finally choose not to adopt the Silent Way, we will sharpen our own skills as teachers if we learn to use it.

7 Humanistic elements outside the 'humanistic' methods

7.1 Humanism in two of the 'humanisms'

This book has not been intended as an encyclopedia of the 'humanistic' approaches to language teaching. It has attempted only to look at humanism in relation to the field of language teaching, and at the ways in which what has been called 'humanism' has been discussed within that field. Accordingly, we have examined in detail the approaches - the basic thinking - behind only those two 'humanistic' methods that this writer knows most intimately: Community Language Learning and the Silent Way.

Those two approaches are alike in that: (1) each emphasizes some *uniquely human attributes* of the learner; (2) each affirms and promotes human *freedom*, and (3) each contributes in some way to the human *dignity* of the learner. As we saw in Chapters 5 and 6, however, the various 'humanistic' approaches differ, sharply and instructively, in just how they do these three things. Counseling-Learning develops insights about affect (used here as a rough synonym for emotions and feelings) and it emphasizes community. In these respects it concentrates on what in Chapter 2 we called H1 and H2. Gattegno's Science of Education, by contrast, is more concerned with what he calls 'affectivity' - the responsible use of available intellectual energy for the building of new inner resources and awarenesses (H3 and H4). The freedom most conspicuous in Counseling-Learning is internal - 'redemption' from conflicts between the 'I' and the 'myself'. This freedom develops with the support of the 'incarnate' knower and of one's fellow learners. The freedom about which Gattegno talks most, on the other hand, is from one's less-than-fully-human past, and from carried-over traditions, whether derived from past generations or from one's own previous conclusions. As for dignity, Curran seemed to see it in the individual's participation in community. For Gattegno, although the fully human person is a loving and constructive member of society, basic dignity is still that of the lone, questing individual moving from life to life in pursuit of ever-growing awareness.

7.2 Humanistic elements in other approaches

It may be useful to look briefly at these same three aspects of seven additonal approaches which are not normally considered to be 'humanistic'. One of the seven, AudioLingualism, is classified by Diller (1978) as 'empiricist' in its view of learning. The principal doctrines of 'empiricist' language teaching, according to Diller, are that learning is the formation of muscular speech habits, that those habits are to be shaped through selective reinforcement of student responses, and that accuracy must be achieved before fluency is attempted. This kind of teaching therefore emphasizes rote memorization of dialogs and mechanical manipulation of structure drills.

The other six approaches at which we shall look are Grammar-Translation, the Direct Method of de Sauzé, Total Physical Response, the Natural Approach, Suggestopedia, and the Communicative Approach. All of these in one way or another fall within Diller's 'rationalist' category, with emphasis on the mind's ability to formulate and use 'rules' of various kinds. Except for Grammar-Translation, these are also approaches in which learners meet new language in the context of challenging, interesting activities - another characteristic which Diller ascribes to 'rationalist' teaching.

We will ask three questions about each of these seven approaches:

☐ Which *uniquely human attributes* of the learner does this approach emphasize?
☐ What sort of *freedom* does this approach offer to the learner?
☐ How does this method contribute to human *dignity*?

By pointing out these qualities in the approaches mentioned above, we may hope to sharpen the distinction between the various aspects of humanism (2.2.2, 2.4, and 2.5) on the one hand and, on the other, 'humanism' as a mere label applied to this or that approach to language teaching.

7.2.1 Uniquely human attributes
The first of our three questions is 'Which *uniquely human attributes* of the learner does this approach emphasize?'

Grammar-Translation
Grammar-Translation emphasizes *the ability of the human mind to reason and to decipher*, and *the ability of the human spirit to persevere*. These are the main ingredients of the 'mental discipline' that has often been said to

accrue through the study of classical languages. This feature of Grammar-Translation has brought many students into Latin classes over the years.

AudioLingualism

'Empiricist' AudioLingualism emphasizes *the ability of the human nervous system to acquire new speech habits through physical practice, and to analogize from existing habits so as to create new behavior on the basis of old, well-established behavior.*

de Sauzé's Direct Method

The 'rationalist' Direct Method of de Sauzé, as Diller describes it, emphasizes *the ability of the human mind to formulate rules and follow them.* But we must take into account the fact that 'rule' has at least two separate meanings (Diller 1978, p.27). Unfortunately, these two meanings have often been used side-by-side in discussions of language learning. If by a 'rule' we mean an explicit, verbalized statement about how to do things, then the empiricist answer of AudioLingualism and the rationalist answer of the Direct Method are quite different from each other. The two answers differ much less if the rationalist's 'rule' stands for any regularity, whether or not that regularity is explicitly formulated or formulatable, and if the empiricist's 'acquiring a new speech habit' means becoming able to respond to and reproduce a regularity that has not not hitherto been responded to or reproduced.

Total Physical Response

As its name implies, Total Physical Response places more emphasis than other methods on *the link between words and actions.* There is, however, more to the approach than just following directions to 'jump to the door' and so on, for the actions themselves depend in turn on perceptions, and on judgments drawn from those perceptions, and on decisions influenced by those judgments. Except for the simplest aspects of perception, all of these represent uniquely human capabilities.

The Natural Approach

The Natural Approach makes free and creative use of the ideas and techniques of Total Physical Response. In addition, it exploits three facts about human nature:

- ☐ Adults as well as infants have significant ability to benefit from informal, gradual learning ('*acquisition*').
- ☐ *Emotional factors* can influence the learning and use of language (the so-called 'affective filter').
- ☐ Human beings are able to '*monitor*' their own language, but they are also able to use language without 'monitoring' it.

Suggestopedia

Among the unique human characteristics emphasized by Suggestopedia, the best-publicized has been the 'reserve powers of the mind' - the ability to learn many times more rapidly and more retentively than is generally believed possible. This is sometimes called '*hypermnesia*'. A second characteristic, on which hypermnesia in fact depends, is the possibility of '*infantilisation*' - of helping even older adults to reach a child-like state in class. More fundamental still is the way in which humans respond to subtle cues that are outside their central awareness. This is the means by which 'infantilisation' is achieved. It is also the source of the name '*Suggest*opedia'.

The Communicative Approach

Perhaps the most characteristically human emphasis of the Communicative Approach is on *the relationship*, not only between sentences and meanings, but also - and more important - *between discourse and life*. Students are given reasons for communicating, not just instructions on how to communicate should they ever need to. This emphasis places a high premium on *social and mental reality* - on genuineness - so much so that even interpersonal elements in an activity, a role-play for example, are to be avoided if they are spurious. As in Widdowson's 'discourse-to-discourse' scheme (1978, p.145ff.), such a methodology starts with communicative native-speaker discourse, and goes on to provide exercises which challenge learners to do their own communicating. (See also Brumfit 1979, and Allwright 1979.)

7.2.2 Freedom

The second question is, 'What sort of *freedom* does this method offer to a learner?'

Grammar-Translation

Grammar-Translation offers *freedom from the limitations of one's own local and contemporary culture*. This has been another common inducement for taking four years of Latin, or even for taking two.

AudioLingualism

AudioLingualism offers *freedom (1) from the requirement to manipulate abstractions for the deciphering and production of sentences - sentences whose meaning at worst is trivial, and at best is distant in time, space, and culture from the interests of the learner*, and *(2) from the requirement to memorize rules and paradigms*.

de Sauzé's Direct Method
The Direct Method of de Sauzé offers freedom (1) *from the requirement to repeat sentences and dialogs for non-communicative purposes*, and (2) *from the requirement to memorize sentences and dialogs*.

Total Physical Response
Like the Direct Method, Total Physical Response gives the learner freedom *from meaninglessness*. It also brings freedom *from having to sit still most of the time*.

The Natural Approach
With its emphasis on 'acquisition' rather than on 'learning', the Natural Approach frees both learner and teacher from *having to be immediately and continuously concerned with correct production of individual features of grammar and pronunciation*. (This freedom is also implied in the practice of Total Physical Response.)

Suggestopedia
Like AudioLingualism and like the Direct Method, Suggestopedia liberates the learner from *the requirement to memorize* either rules or paradigms or dialogs, even though memorization or near-memorization of dialogs may actually take place in the famous 'concert pseudopassive' sessions. Suggestopedia also - and uniquely - frees learners from *uncomfortable physical surroundings*. Most important, it liberates them from the *limiting and often negative suggestions* that permeate many classrooms.

The Communicative Approach
Some approaches start with a set of component skills in pronunciation, vocabulary, and grammar, and build from them to (or toward) discourse. Others begin with examples of discourse and reduce it either to its elements or to a translation. In the Communicative Approach, instruction ideally moves from discourse by established writers or speakers to discourse by the learners themselves - from a reading passage to class discussion, for example. Whatever relatively mechanical drills and exercises may still be necessary are justified by the contribution they make to the transition from one of these discourses to the other. Students are therefore largely freed from *artificiality* - from having to do with the foreign language something that they are not normally required to do with their native language. This in turn means that they are freed from *wasted effort* - from learning a great deal that will be of no value to them once they have left the classroom.

7.2.3 Dignity

The third question is 'How does this approach contribute to human *dignity*?'

Grammar-Translation

The aim of Grammar-Translation is to place the mind of the student *in direct contact with the words and with the ideas of great thinkers of classical times.* This is no small goal, and when it is achieved it is no small achievement.

AudioLingualism

AudioLingualism, in contrast to Grammar-Translation, *encourages the learner to produce language for his or her own purposes, rather than just absorbing the ideas of others.* Although AudioLingual study begins with memorization of the words of others (the basic dialogs), its eventual goal is face-to-face communication, something that Grammar-Translation does not even attempt.

de Sauzé's Direct Method

The Direct Method of de Sauzé, in contrast to AudioLingualism, *encourages the learner to use his or her own mind, rather than being treated as a mindless 'nervous system' whose acts are merely the results of complex sequences of causes and effects* (Bloomfield 1933, p.33). Diller quotes, with apparent approval, de Sauzé's opinion that learning is most efficient when it makes maximum use of conscious reasoning.

Total Physical Response

More than any of its predecessors, Total Physical Response assures teachers and students that *it's all right to have a little fun while learning.*

The Natural Approach

In addition to liberating students from the demand for immediate correctness, the Natural Approach requires that students be given large quantities of comprehensible input. This opens the way for language instruction that *credits learners with being adults intellectually,* even while it recognizes them as linguistic infants.

Suggestopedia

In its practice of assigning fictitious identities to its learners, Suggestopedia treats them as *successful, prestigious, even slightly glamorous characters who are free of serious internal conflicts* rather than as tired bureaucrats or factory workers who are trying to learn a language through obedience to a traditional teacher.

The Communicative Approach
In the Communicative Approach, learners are led to recognize that the tasks they are asked to undertake relate to the way they use their own language for the achievement of genuine communicative purposes. As in the Natural Approach, *their intellectual and social maturity is taken into account*. One pioneer in this approach reported that many learners *value being prompted, and trusted, to make a more 'substantial contribution to their own learning* (Allwright 1979).

7.3 'Empiricism' and 'rationalism' in language teaching

Diller's contrast between 'empiricist' and 'rationalist' approaches deserves a little more attention before we bring this investigation of humanism in language teaching to a close.

7.3.1 Empiricism and humanism
The main principles of what Diller calls 'empiricist' teaching stand out clearly in the AudioLingual Method. Those principles are: (1) formation of muscular speech habits; (2) shaping of those habits through selective reinforcement of student responses; (3) use of the native language for translation of basic material and for explanation of structure, and (4) accuracy before fluency. The most characteristic technique of AudioLingualism is massive repetition of dialogs or grammar drills or both, with the goal of memorizing the former and achieving unthinking automaticity in responding to the latter.

'Rationalist' teaching, as Diller describes it in the Direct Method, sees language learning as the recognition, formation, and use of rules of various kinds. Students meet the new language in a carefully graded sequence of vocabulary and structures, always in the context of challenging, interesting activities.

The kinds of freedom listed in 7.2.2 are matters of classroom activity only. But the empiricists from whom AudioLingualism was derived (7.2) saw themselves as bringers of a more important kind of freedom. In the areas of philosophy and religion, the secular humanistic vision (2.5) had provided an alternative to previously unchallenged doctrines about incorporeal beings - doctrines which were based on writings in the classical languages of Hebrew, Greek, and Latin. Now, in the area of language, the empiricists working as descriptive linguists were providing an alternative to incorporeal categories and theories that had become parts of accepted tradition, and freedom from the idea that all languages should be analyzed in terms of the structures of those same classical languages, especially Latin.

As in the area of linguistic analysis, so also in the area of usage, the empiricists were bringers of freedom. They liked to say that their approach to language was 'descriptive, not prescriptive'. Rules of speech and writing, like dogmas of theology and standards of conduct, were no longer in the hands of a small class of powerful specialists who interpreted tradition according to their own best lights - and perhaps also according to their own interests (Loveday 1982). Instead, guides for usage were to be drawn from the everyday life - the everyday speech - of the people.

In both these areas, then, the empiricists considered themselves iconoclasts - smashers of ancient idols. Diller (1978, p.18) rightly points out that in their zeal they went to unwarranted extremes in some of their statements. But in their intentions, and to some extent in fact, they were liberators. This was the humanism of the responsible intellect (H3 and H4 in 2.2.2). Its defect, as we saw in the remarks on the question about dignity, was that it went too far in one direction and not far enough in another.

With its uncompromising focus on external forms, and with its adamant refusal to work with intuition-based categories or analyses (see 7.2.2), the empiricists' approach proved a valuable tool - a tool by which disciplined investigators were able to discover something of what was actually present in language. Armed with these new observations, people could challenge whatever explanations, whatever theories, whatever hypotheses, whatever 'conjectures' (1.2.2 to 1.2.3), the upholders of tradition might try to force upon them.

The categories and theories against which the empiricists rebelled had two characteristics:

- ☐ They had been derived from intuition - from more-or-less skilled guesswork - rather than from disciplined observation of a body of data.

- ☐ They had not been checked against publicly accessible data.

That is to say, the empiricists objected both to the *source* of the categories and theories, and to *what had (not) been done with those categories and theories*. The great contribution of the empiricists was that they worked out with unprecedented rigor a series of methods for sticking to data - to data that are publicly accessible - and for checking analyses *against* those data. The descriptive linguists thus eliminated one characteristic of the categories and theories to which they were objecting: that they had not been checked. But they also tried to derive their new categories and theories *from* those same data and methods without resorting to intuition or guesswork. In this way they hoped to avoid creating new analyses that would be as subject to criticism as the old analyses had been.

Unfortunately, the verbalized categories and theories that could be devised within these restrictions were unable to represent with any clarity an important number of the regularities that are found in the languages of the world (7.2.1, de Sauzé's Direct Method). What the empiricists had not noticed was that, although the theories against which they rightly objected had *both* of the characteristics listed above - that is, they had been derived from intuition *and* they had not been checked against data - only *one* of those characteristics was a flaw, i.e. the fact that the theories had not been checked against potentially falsifying data. The fault for continued acceptance of a defective theory lies not with the introspection that produced the theory, but with the failure to test it. This is consistent with Popper's scientific approach, described in 1.2.

The new breed of rationalists who challenged the empiricists had learned from the empiricists how to gather publicly accessible data. But the rationalists were willing *both* to use introspection as a source for their conjectures, *and* to conjecture about entities that were abstract and inaccessible to direct observation. This was what enabled the rationalists to produce richer and more satisfying analyses than their predecessors had ever arrived at. *What must be subjected to public scrutiny is neither the content of a conjecture nor its source, but only its results.* Or so Popper seems to be saying (1.2). The empiricists saw that products of unchecked imagination can be misleading and destructive. Their response was to confine imagination within the narrowest possible limits. The rationalists, by allowing a much wider range for imagination, developed the intellectual side of humanism (H4) without sacrificing the side that values responsibility (H3).

The preceding paragraphs are about the empiricists as linguistic scientists. But as often happens, the science of linguistics was taken as a model for the art and science of language teaching. The empiricists' avowedly materialistic and mechanistic view, with its distrust of imagination and with its insistence on talking only about 'nervous systems' and never about 'minds' (Bloomfield 1933, p.33ff.), led them to the conclusion that learning can only take place as a response to external stimuli, and that teaching must therefore consist in the nervous system of the teacher-organism selecting and arranging the stimuli to which the nervous systems of the learner-organisms are to be subjected (Brooks 1961). Though Cornelius (1953) and Brooks (1961) urged teachers trained in the empiricist method to exercise 'the greatest liberty' in their choice of materials and methods, memorization and pattern drill were still very clearly the most convenient means for putting their methods into action.

7.3.2 'Rationalism' and some methods labeled 'humanistic'

Diller clearly finds in favor of the rationalist rather than the empiricist point of view. In spite of my occasional remarks in defense of some uses of mimicry, memorization, and pattern drills, I generally agree with him. In his chapter on trends that in 1978 were new, Diller (1978) lists three characteristics of the Direct Method which seem also to represent for him the core of rationalist practice in language teaching. These three characteristics are: (1) avoidance of the mother tongue; (2) following a step-by-step progression in grammar, and (3) meaningful practice. Diller also notes that (4) rationalist teaching does not adhere so rigidly as empiricist teaching to the slogan 'Hearing before Speaking, Speaking before Reading, Reading before Writing'.

Of these four principles, Diller says that 'meaningful practice is ... regarded by many to be the key to effective language teaching' (1978, pp.143, 146), in contrast to the empiricists' insistence on postponing meaningful practice until after learning has already been accomplished through mimicry, memorization, and drills. Diller finds that Community Language Learning (see Chapter 5) and the Silent Way (see Chapter 6) are generally 'compatible with rationalist-cognitivist theories' (1978, p.143). Of course, there is probably no method that is purely 'empiricist' or purely 'rationalist'. For example, in his comments on Community Language Learning, Diller concedes that that method does not avoid the student's mother tongue, or follow a pre-set grammatical progression. And as I last saw Silent Way practiced, there were short periods between the main sessions, still parts of the course, when students were encouraged to talk in their native language about whatever tentative conclusions they had reached in working with the charts or with the rods. If Diller were writing the same book today he would also have to note that the very non-empiricist Natural Approach emphasizes the empiricists' watchword 'Hearing before Speaking' to an extent undreamed of by the empiricists, and that the Natural Approach also denies the value of introducing grammatical points one by one in a fixed sequence. Diller's main point still stands, however: all of the newer methods employ large amounts of practice that in one way or another is meaningful rather than mechanical.

Perhaps the great fundamental tenet of the rationalists, underlying all four of the principles listed above, is:

> Within each student there is a mind. This mind is active, constantly generating hypotheses within a genetically determined range, testing those hypotheses against what comes in from the outside world, and modifying its hypotheses according to the results of its tests.

According to the rationalists, then, we teachers are free to say things to our students that we know they will have to figure out: 'figuring out' is, after all, an activity for which our students, as human beings, are innately equipped. We do not have to say with Cornelius (1953) that 'students cannot be expected to answer questions or [to] use the foreign language without first having learned the questions and answers through observation, imitation, and continued repetition' (p.132).

The corresponding tenet of the empiricists is:

> Within each student there is a nervous system. That nervous system is constantly responsive to external stimuli. Its likelihood of reacting in one way or another can be modified by careful management of the stimuli to which that nervous system is exposed, and of the reactions which the external environment gives to the student's behavior.

The existence of the nervous system is not a matter of controversy, and the possibility of shaping certain kinds of behavior has been demonstrated beyond doubt. Thus, the first graduate of Rand Morton's programmed instruction in Spanish was sent immediately to Mexico, where he was taken for a native-speaking ignoramus. This was, of course, exactly the result that Morton had hoped to obtain. Equally significant, though, this same student quickly learned enough content in Spanish so that he was invited back to Mexico the following summer as a university instructor in psychology.

Some theorists have appeared to believe that the empiricist tenet is both sufficient and necessary for understanding how a second language is acquired and for planning how to teach it. I think they are wrong. Other theorists seem to deny that the empiricist tenet has any relevance at all to second language acquisition and would exclude it from thinking about methodology. I think they are wrong too.

7.3.3 Three general insights from Diller

Diller ends his comments on the unconventional newer methods, including the methods that have been called 'humanistic', with three observations that have not gone out of date and never will. One is that each of these methods has been the result of taking one or two very sharply defined principles and, in a phrase of Gouin's quoted by Diller, 'following [those principles] long and far' (1978, p.150). Many of the devisers of unconventional methods have been people from outside the language teaching profession: Asher an experimental psychologist, Curran a clinical psychologist, Gattegno a mathematician and general student of education, Lozanov a psychiatrist. Their positions as outsiders have allowed them to come up with 'brilliant insights' (p.148) that had never before been systematically exploited within the language teaching profession, and for this we must be grateful to them. But as outsiders they also designed methods that do not take into account the full range of social and curricular realities within which most language teaching is done. For that matter, one could say much the same thing about the methods of the empiricists, i.e. that those methods originated with ideas from people (behavioral psychologists and descriptive linguists) who were outside the language teaching profession, and that the same methods followed two limited insights (the potential value of involving the speech muscles in mechanical practice, and the effect of simple overt reinforcement) so 'long and far' that they came to have the flaws that Diller and others have criticized.

Second, Diller observes that 'it is possible to learn a great deal from [an] unusual and unconventional method ... without necessarily adopting any recognizable feature of the method' (p.150). I emphatically agree with Diller here, although unlike Diller I can find at least two of those methods that I would be very happy to follow with a real class. Perhaps this difference between Diller and me is due to the fact that, writing in 1978, Diller seemed not to realize the extent to which it is possible to enrich most of those unconventional methods without departing from them. Thus we saw in Chapter 5 that the conversational circle of Community Language Learning was not the method: it was only the prototypical technique of that method. But during the years I was working with Community Language Learning, many new and superficially quite different techniques were either originated by teachers or borrowed from other methods and integrated into Community Language Learning. Similarly, we saw in Chapter 6 that the essence of the Silent Way does not lie in wallcharts or in cuisenaire rods, or even in the silence of the teacher. And in spite of Lozanov's warnings against methodological tinkering, a number of his followers in various parts of the world have come up with quite a range of effective variations on the original Suggestopedia.

Third, and perhaps most important, Diller points out that it is possible to borrow techniques from the unconventional methods without really learning anything from them. Needless to say, borrowing should always be done with the intention of better meeting the needs of an ongoing class, but it should at the same time be done with judgment, taking into account the kinds of principles that Diller outlined.

7.4 Summary of this book

Often, it seems, we are drawn to this method or to that model for a variety of reasons. Those reasons may include one or another of its by-products. That is to say, the method or the model may, through its impressive results, appear to confirm some conclusion that we had already wanted to reach. These desired conclusions are important elements of our 'faith', in the general sense in which that word has been used in this book (1.3.4). Examples of such conclusions are:

- ☐ Kindness is more effective than coercion.
- ☐ Firmness is more effective than permissiveness.
- ☐ When students feel good about the course and about themselves, they will learn better than when they do not.
- ☐ Any method that does not require serious and occasionally onerous effort from learners will be ineffective.
- ☐ Within us (or within our grasp) we have undreamed-of possibilities.
- ☐ Concentrated, intuitive introspection together with courage and patience will make possible unlimited growth in constructive and socially desirable directions.
- ☐ Skilled and sensitive understanding of another person can release that other person's whole self so it can deal adequately with whatever needs to be dealt with, whether cognitive or otherwise.
- ☐ Rational, critical inquiry can deal adequately with everything that really needs to be dealt with.
- ☐ A model of teaching (or thinking) which makes full use of one's own personal strengths is superior to models which demand strengths of other kinds. (Corollary: a model which demands strength in an area where one is weak is misguided.)

There is one more conclusion - a sort of meta-conclusion - that crops up frequently. (I heard a further very clear example of it just the evening before I finished the revision of this chapter.) It is that whoever has not accepted the model of teaching (or thinking) which one has adopted at great cost to oneself is either ignorant or dishonest or both, but in any case is probably dangerous.

Discussions of 'humanism' in language teaching, this writer's included, have for the most part been unsatisfactory for a number of reasons:

☐ Too often, *by-products of the discussion have been implicit and unrecognized. When they are unrecognized, they are capable of causing either intellectual confusion or intense emotion or both.* Popper has taught us that participants in discussion, defenders and opponents alike, should be careful both in using words and in responding to the words of others (Chapter 1).

☐ *The word 'humanism' itself has been treated as though it had a single meaning*, when in fact it has several (Chapter 2).

☐ *Confusion can result when a word has been chosen because of some part of its meaning, but other parts of its meaning have come in along with the intended part.* 'Level', 'depth', and 'filter' are such words, along with 'humanism' itself (Chapter 3).

☐ *Undesired complications can also arise when a discussant even inadvertently uses language which suggests something that he or she has not said explicitly.* Indirect derogatory intimation, use of emotionally loaded words, and syllogistic fallacies are examples of this (Chapter 4).

☐ *Some of the undesired complications are feelings of the kinds that Alan Maley in Honolulu called 'religious'.* Throughout this book, we have dealt explicitly with these aspects of the discussion wherever they have come up.

☐ *Too few discussants have had sufficient access to what the 'humanistic' innovators were saying in the first place - to their 'world-3 objects'.* In Chapters 5 and 6 we have tried to remedy this lack, at least for Counseling-Learning and the Silent Way, and also to locate those two methods in relation to the various meanings of 'humanism'.

Overall, our intention in this book has been neither to promote 'humanism' in language teaching nor to discourage it - neither to attack nor to defend any form of it. Instead, we have tried to sort out a few terms and the ideas that have sometimes been attached to them, and to provide certain new information. It is hoped that what has been done here will make it easier for others in the profession to examine more fully, and in Popper's sense more critically, the 'humanistic' - and even the humanistic - aspects of language teaching.

Bibliography

Allibone, S.A. 1876. *Prose Quotations.* Philadelphia, Pa.: Lippincott.

Allport, G.W. and **L. Postman.** 1947. *The Psychology of Rumor.* New York: Holt.

Allwright, R. 1979. 'Language learning through communication practice' in Brumfit and Johnson (eds.) 1979.

American College Dictionary. 1960. New York: Random House.

Anthony, E.A. 1963. 'Approach, method, and technique.' *English Language Teaching* 17/2.

Auden, W.H. 1957. 'Horae Canonicae: vespers' in *Selected poems of W.H. Auden.* New York: The Modern Library.

Bhanot, R. 1983. Review of Early (ed.) 1982. *English Language Teaching Journal* 37/4.

Bloomfield, L. 1933. *Language.* New York: Holt.

Bodman, J. and **M. Lanzano.** 1975. *No Hot Water Tonight.* New York: Collier Macmillan.

Bolitho, R. 1982. 'CLL: a way forward?' in Early (ed.) 1982.

Bransford, J.D. 1979. *Human Cognition.* Belmont, Calif.: Wadsworth.

Breen, M.P. 1987. 'Contemporary programs in syllabus design: Part II.' *Language Teaching* 20/3.

Brooks, N. 1960. *Language and Language Learning.* New York: Harcourt-Brace.

Brown, H.D. 1980. *Principles of Language Learning and Language Teaching.* Englewood Cliffs, NJ: Prentice-Hall.

Brumfit, C.J. 1979. ' "Communicative" language teaching: an educational perspective' in Brumfit and Johnson (eds.) 1979.

Brumfit, C.J. 1982a. 'Some humanistic doubts about humanistic language teaching' in Early (ed.) 1982.

Brumfit, C.J. 1982b. 'Alternative teaching strategies and conventional education.' Reprinted in Brumfit 1985.

Brumfit, C.J. 1984. *Communicative Methodology in Language Teaching: The Roles of Fluency and Accuracy.* Cambridge: Cambridge University Press.

Brumfit, C.J. 1985. *Language and Literature Teaching: From Practice to Principle.* Oxford: Pergamon.

Brumfit, C.J. and **K. Johnson.** (eds.) 1979. *The Communicative Approach to Language Teaching.* Oxford: Oxford University Press.

Butts, R.F. 1964. 'Humanities', in *The World Book Encyclopedia Dictionary.* Chicago, Ill.: Field Enterprises.

Buxton, L. 1981. *Do You Panic About Maths? Coping with Maths Anxiety.* London: Heinemann.

Clarke, M.A. 1982. 'On bandwagons, tyranny and common sense.' *TESOL Quarterly* 16/4.

Clarke, M.A. and **J. Handscombe.** (eds.) 1983. *On TESOL '82: Pacific Perspectives on Language Learning and Teaching.* Washington, DC: TESOL.

Clifford, B.R. and **C.R. Hollin.** 1981. 'Effects of the type of incident and the number of perpetrators on eyewitness memory.' *Journal of Applied Psycholinguistics* 66/3.

Cornelius, E.T., Jr. 1953. *Language Teaching: A Guide for Teachers of Foreign Languages.* New York: Crowell.

Craik, F.I.M. 1973. 'A levels of analysis view of memory' in Pliner *et al.* (eds.) 1973.

Craik, F.I.M. and **R.S. Lockhart.** 1972. 'Levels of processing: a framework for memory research.' *Journal of Verbal Learning and Verbal Behavior* 2.

Curran, C.A. 1968. *Counseling and Psychotherapy: The Pursuit of Values.* New York: Sheed and Ward.

Curran, C.A. 1972a. *Counseling-Learning: A Whole-Person Model for Education.* New York: Grune and Stratton.

Curran, C.A. 1972b. *Learning: An Incarnate-Redemptive Self-Investment Process.* Apple River, Ill.: Counseling-Learning Institutes.

Curran, C.A. 1976. *Counseling-Learning in Second Languages.* Apple River, Ill.: Apple River Press.

Curran, C.A. 1978. *Understanding: A Necessary Ingredient in Human Belonging.* Apple River, Ill.: Apple River Press.

Deutsch, B. 1974. *Poetry Handbook: A Dictionary of Terms.* New York: Funk and Wagnalls.

Diller, K.C. 1978. *The Language Teaching Controversy.* Rowley, Mass.: Newbury House.

Dulay, H., M. Burt, and **S.D. Krashen.** 1982. *Language Two.* Oxford: Oxford University Press.

Early, P. (ed.) 1982. *Humanistic Approaches: An Empirical View.* London: The British Council.

Easterbrook, J.A. 1959. 'The effect of emotion on cue utilization and the organization of behavior.' *Psychological Review* 66/3.

Elbow, P. 1973. *Writing without Teachers.* New York: Oxford University Press.

Ellis, R. 1988. *Classroom Second Language Development.* Hemel Hempstead: Prentice Hall International.

Fowler, H.W. 1940. *A Dictionary of Modern English Usage.* London: Oxford University Press.

Galyean, B. 1977. 'A confluent design for language teaching.' *TESOL Quarterly* 11/2.

Gattegno, C. 1962. *The Adolescent and His Self.* Reading, Mass.: Educational Explorers Limited.

Gattegno, C. 1972. *Teaching Foreign Languages in Schools: The Silent Way.* (Revised edition.) New York: Educational Solutions Inc.

Gattegno, C. 1973. *In the Beginning There Were No Words: The Universe of Babies.* New York: Educational Solutions Inc.

Gattegno, C. 1975a. *On Being Freer.* (First edition.) New York: Educational Solutions Inc.

Gattegno, C. 1975b. *The Mind Teaches the Brain.* New York: Educational Solutions Inc.

Gattegno, C. 1976a. *The Common Sense of Teaching Foreign Languages.* New York: Educational Solutions Inc.

Gattegno, C. 1976b. 'On mistakes' in *Educational Solutions Newsletter* 6/2-3.

Gattegno, C. 1977a. *On Love.* New York: Educational Solutions Inc.

Gattegno, C. 1977b. *Evolution and Memory.* New York: Educational Solutions Inc.

Gattegno, C. 1978. *On Death.* New York: Educational Solutions Inc.

Gattegno, C. 1979. *Who Cares about Health?* New York: Educational Solutions Inc.

Gattegno, C. 1985a. 'The learning and teaching of foreign languages.' (Reprinted as Chapter 13 of *The Science of Education.*)

Gattegno, C. 1985b. *The Common Sense of Teaching Reading and Writing.* New York: Educational Solutions Inc.

Gattegno, C. 1986. 'Memory and retention.' (Reprinted as Chapter 5 of *The Science of Education.*)

Gattegno, C. 1987. *The Science of Education. Part 1: Theoretical Considerations.* New York: Educational Solutions Inc.

Gattegno, C. 1988a. *On Being Freer.* (Revised edition.) New York: Educational Solutions Inc.

Gattegno, C. 1988b. *The Mind Teaches the Brain.* (Revised edition.) New York: Educational Solutions Inc.

Glucksberg, S. and **J.H. Danks.** 1975. *Experimental Psycholinguistics: An Introduction.* Hillsdale, NJ: Lawrence Erlbaum.

Guiora, A.Z. 1972. 'Construct validity and transpositional research: toward an empirical study of psychoanalytical concepts.' *Comprehensive Psychiatry* 13/5.

Guiora, A.Z. 1983. 'The dialectic of language acquisition.' *Language Learning* 33/5.

Guiora, A.Z., M. Paluszny, B. Beit-Hallahmi, J.C. Catford, R.E. Colley, and **C.Y. Dull.** 1975. 'Language and person: studies in language behavior.' *Language Learning* 25/1.

Hall, N.F. and **L.K.B. Hall.** 1986. 'Is the war between science and religion over?' *The Humanist* 46/26-8.

Harris, E.L. 1986. 'Snow as a literary image for a schizophrenic state.' *Journal of Mental Imagery* 10/2.

Harris, T.A. 1967. *I'm OK - You're OK.* New York: Harper and Row.

Hollin, C.R. 1984. 'Arousal and eyewitness memory.' *Perceptual and Motor Skills* 58.

Jakobovits, LA. and **B. Gordon.** 1974. *The Context of Foreign Language Teaching.* Rowley, Mass.: Newbury House.

Kattsoff, L.O. 1964. 'Humanism' in *The World Book Encyclopedia Dictionary.* Chicago, Ill.: Field Enterprises.

Koffman, E.B. and **F.L. Friedman.** 1979. *Problem Solving and Structured Programming in Basic.* Reading, Mass.: Addison-Wesley.

Krashen, S.D. 1981. *Second Language Learning and Second Language Acquisition.* Oxford: Pergamon.

Krashen, S.D. 1982. *Principles and Practice in Second Language Acquisition.* Oxford: Pergamon.

Krashen, S.D. and **T.D. Terrell.** 1983. *The Natural Approach: Language Acquisition in the Classroom.* Oxford: Pergamon.

Kurtz, P. 1973. *The Humanistic Alternative: Some Definitions of Humanism.* London: Pemberton.

Küng, H. 1966. *On Being a Christian.* New York: Doubleday.

Larsen-Freeman, D. 1986. *Techniques and Principles in Language Teaching.* Oxford and New York: Oxford University Press.

Larson, D.N. and **W.A. Smalley.** 1984. *Becoming Bilingual: A Guide to Language Learning.* Lanham, MD: University Press of America.

Lewis, C.S. 1943. *Mere Christianity*. London: Macmillan.

Lott, A.J., B.E. Lott, and **M.L. Walsh.** 1970. 'Learning of paired associates relative to differentially-liked persons.' *Journal of Personal and Social Psychology* 16.

Loveday, L. 1982. *The Sociolinguistics of Learning and Using a Non-native Language*. Oxford: Pergamon.

Lozanov, G. 1979. *Suggestology and Outlines of Suggestopedy*. New York: Gordon and Breach.

Maley, A. 1983. 'I got religion!: evangelism in TEFL' in Clarke and Handscombe (eds.) 1983.

Maples, M.F. 1979. 'A humanistic education: basic ingredients.' *The Humanistic Educator* 17/3.

McNeill, A. 1982. 'The Silent Way: evaluating an experience' in Early (ed.) 1982.

Medgyes, P. 1986. 'Queries from a communicative teacher.' *English Language Teaching Journal* 40/2.

More, Thomas. (1516.) *Utopia. Harvard Classics* Vol. 36. New York: Collier.

Morris, C.D., J.D. Bransford, and **J.J. Franks.** 1977. 'Levels of processing versus transfer appropriate processing.' *Journal of Verbal Learning and Verbal Behavior* 16.

Moskowitz, G. 1978. *Caring and Sharing in the Foreign Language Class: A Sourcebook on Humanistic Techniques*. Rowley, Mass.: Newbury House.

Oller, J. 1983. Editor's introduction to the chapter on 'Counseling-Learning' in Oller and Richard-Amato (eds.) 1983.

Oller, J. and **P.A. Richard-Amato.** 1983. *Methods that Work: A Smorgasbord of Ideas for Language Teachers*. Rowley: Mass.: Newbury House.

Oxford English Dictionary. (Compact edition) 1971. Oxford: Oxford University Press.

Perecman, E. 1984. 'Spontaneous translation and language mixing in a polyglot aphasic.' *Brain and Language* 23.

Pliner, P., L. Kramer, and **T. Alloway.** (eds.) 1973. *Communication and Affect: Language and Thought*. New York: Academic Press.

Pope, Alexander. (1734.) *An Essay on Man. Harvard Classics* Vol. 1. New York: Collier.

Popper, K. 1976. *Unended Quest*. Glasgow: Collins.

Richards, J. 1985. *The Context of Language Teaching.* Cambridge:
    Cambridge University Press.
Richards, J. and **T. Rodgers.** 1982. 'Method, approach, design and
    procedure.' TESOL *Quarterly* 16/2.
Richards, J. and **T. Rodgers.** (eds.) 1986. *Approaches and Methods in
    Language Teaching: A Description and Analysis.* Cambridge:
    Cambridge University Press.
Rivers, W. 1983. *Communicating Naturally in a Second Language:
    Theory and Practice in Language Teaching.* Cambridge: Cambridge
    University Press.
Roberts, J.T. 1982. 'Recent developments in ELT.' *Language Teaching*
    15/2 - 3.
Roberts, R.C. 1985. 'Carl Rogers' quiet revolution.' *Christianity Today*
    29/16.
Rogers, C.R. 1961. *On Becoming a Person.* Boston: Houghton-Mifflin.

Sacks, O. 1984. *A Leg to Stand On.* New York: Summit.
Sampson, G. 1987. Review article on McClelland *et al.*: *Parallel
    Distributed Processing. Language* 63/4.
Scovel, T. 1979. Review of G. Lozanov: *Suggestology and Outlines of
    Suggestopedy. TESOL Quarterly* 13/2.
Scovel, T. 1983. 'Emphasizing language: a reply to Humanism,
    Neoaudiolingualism, and Notional-Functionalism' in Clarke and
    Hanscombe (eds.) 1983.
Stevick, E.W. 1976. *Memory, Meaning and Method.* Rowley, Mass.:
    Newbury House.
Stevick, E.W. 1980. *Teaching Languages: A Way and Ways.* Rowley,
    Mass.: Newbury House.
Stevick, E.W. 1982. 'Humanism' in Early (ed.) 1982.
Stevick, E.W. 1986. *Images and Options in the Language Classroom.*
    New York: Cambridge University Press.
Stevick, E.W. 1989. *Success with Foreign Languages: Seven Who
    Achieved It, and What Worked for Them.* Hemel Hempstead: Prentice
    Hall International.

Terrell, T. 1982. 'The Natural Approach to language teaching: an
    update.' *Modern Language Journal* 66/2.
Terrell, T. 1986. 'Acquisition in the Natural Approach: the binding/
    access framework.' *Modern Language Journal* 70/3.

Underhill, N. 1983. 'Commonsense in oral testing: reliability, validity and affective factors' in Clarke and Handscombe (eds.) 1983.

Walters, J. and **Y. Wolf.** 1986. 'Language proficiency: text, content and order effects in narrative recall.' *Language Learning* 36/1.

Widdowson, H.G. 1978. *Teaching Language as Communication.* London: Oxford University Press.

Widdowson, H.G. 1983. *Learning Purpose and Language Use.* London: Oxford University Press.

Wilson V. and **B.S. Wattenmaker.** 1980. *A Guidebook for Teaching Foreign Language.* Boston: Allyn and Bacon.

World Book Encyclopedia Dictionary. 1964. Chicago, Ill.: Field Enterprises.

Index

Some of the entries in this index are terms and expressions used by a particular writer in a specific sense. Where this is the case, the name of the writer has been added in brackets after the entry.

absolutes (Gattegno)   120
abstraction (Gattegno)   109
acquisition (Gattegno) 133, *see also* learning and acquisition
acronyms   37, 38
action, bases for rational (Popper)   10
adhering (Gattegno)   122
adoption of a way of thinking (Popper)   11
adult resistance (Curran)   89
affect   48-9, 131, 133
Affective Filter (metaphor)   48-9, 50, 133
    difficulties with   50
affectivity (Gattegno)   113-14, 131
aim of science (Popper)   9
alienation (Curran)   90
Allibone, S. A.   39
Allport, G. and N. Postman   56
Allwright, R.   134, 137
'Annie Laurie'   36
Anthony, E. A.   19
ARC, *see* attributive and reminiscent connections
Arcadian   29-31, 33, 98, 130
Asher, J.   142
attitude, rational or critical (Popper)   10
attributes
    of stimuli   36
    of the self (Gattegno) 109
    of the student   132-4
attributive and reminiscent connections   36-8, 55-9
Auden, W. H.   29-30, 98, 129

AudioLingualism   133, 134, 135, 136, 137
Augustine of Hippo   65
authoritarianism, a charge against 'humanism'   96
autonomy (Gattegno)   106, 121
awareness   106, 108-9, 115, 129, 131
    of awareness   108, 110
    forcing of   106, 117

babies, as models for learning in the Silent Way   106
'bag' (Gattegno)   115, 129
barriers (implication of metaphors)   54
bases for action (Popper)   11, 14, 17
Beethoven   16
belief (Popper)   10, 11, 13
believing (Gattegno)   122-3
believing game   68
Bhanot, R.   26
black box   35, 43, 51, 53, 128
Bloomfield, L.   136, 139
Bodman, J. and M. Lanzano   71
Bolitho, R.   57
boundaries (implication of metaphors)   43, 44, 46, 53
boundary-barrier metaphor   48
Bransford, J.D.   47
Breen, M. P.   97
Brooks, N.   140
    maxim   13, 97
Brown H. D.   27, 44
Brumfit, C. J. 7,   11, 12, 27, 31, 60, 61, 66, 67, 68, 77, 130, 134
    maxim   19, 20, 97
Butts, R. F.   23
Buxton, L.   64
by-products of models, effects of   143

challenges (Gattegno)   117, 129
'chiseling oneself'   110
Christian theory   77-9, 83-9, 93-5
circularity   20
Clarke, M. A.   69
Clifford, B. R. and C. R. Hollin   49, 50
coercion and exploitation of students   66
cognitive depth   45
commitment (Gattegno)   109
Communicative Approach   134, 135, 137
community   131

Community Language Learning 7, 46, 71, 131, 137, 140, 142
composer's emotions (Popper) 15
conception (Gattegno) 110
confrontation (Curran) 75
congruency 78-9, 83, 86
conjectures (Popper) 9, 12, 138
consciousness (Gattegno) 111-12
constructivist 56
continuity (implication of metaphors) 40, 44
contradiction 9
Cornelius, E. T., Jr. 140, 141
Counseling-Learning 63, 71-99, 126, 129, 131
   and the humanisms 98-9
   feminine elements in 98
   misgivings about 97
   stages in 76
Craik, F. 45, 47
criteria (Gattegno) 117, 123, 128-9
critical attitude (Popper) 12
critical judgment, relation to faith 12
critical method of Popper 9-10
criticism, importance of 9
criticizable though not testable 9
Curran, C. A. 63, 71, 131, 142

Darren 72-7
de Córdoba, C. 112
de Sauzé's Direct Method 133, 135, 136
dead metaphors 36, 39
death 87, 111
debate 55
depth 45, 46, 48, 53
Deutsch, B. 35
dignity 131, 136
Diller, K. C. 133, 136, 137, 138, 140, 142, 143
   three general insights 142
dimension (metaphor) 42, 54
Direct Method 132-3, 135-6, 137, 140
direct variation (implication of metaphors) 42, 44, 46
discarnate (Curran) 74, 79, 90
discipleship (Curran) 91, 94
disconfirmation, a key goal of critical thinking (Popper) 8
discreteness (implication of metaphors) 40, 44
discrimination 9, 109
'doing more with less' (Gattegno) 110

dogma 9, 13
Don 102, 104
Donna 102, 104
Doreen 71-2, 74-5
doubting game, the 68
drama, Science of Education as a 107
Dulay, H., M. Burt, and S. D. Krashen 48, 49, 50, 51, 60

Easterbrook, J. A. 49, 50
education (Gattegno) 116
ego boundaries 51
Einstein, A. 11
emotion 10-12, 18, 49-50, 64, 66, 76, 79, 85, 87, 90, 93, 129
    arousal 49
    loaded vocabulary 55-8, 61
    and music (Popper) 10
empathy 52
empiricists 137, 138, 141
energy and time (Gattegno) 108
energy, quantum of (Gattegno) 109-10
epistemology (Gattegno) 130
ethics (Gattegno) 119, 130
evolution (Gattegno) 109, 122-3, 128
expectation, a step in the method of science (Popper) 9
'exchange time for experience' (Gattegno) 116

'faith' 8, 11-13, 17-18, 20, 30, 54, 63, 85, 97, 99, 128-30, 143
'faith' in relation to critical judgment 12
falsifiability 8, 9, 10, 13, 139
feelings, see emotions
feminine elements in Counseling-Learning 98
'Filter' metaphor, see Affective Filter
forcing awareness (Gattegno) 106, 117
formulation of theories (Popper) 9
freedom 107, 117, 122, 131, 134-5, 137, 138
'fringe methodology' 57

Galyean, B. 31
Gattegno, C. 63, 65, 101, 131, 142
    his view of his own role 123-5
Glucksberg, S. and J. H. Danks 43, 44
gift of the counselor's self 85
god-like position of teacher 89
god-project 80, 89-91
Gouin, F. 142

Grammar-Translation 132, 134, 136
Green, B. 87, 95
Guiora, A. Z. 35, 37, 39, 45, 51-3

habits 133
Hall, N. F. and L. K. B. Hall 22
Harris, E. L. 37
Harris, T. A. 67
'*Heavens Above*' (movie) 80, 88-9, 94-5
Heck, O. 64, 66
hierarchical structure 46
Hollin, C. R. 49
homunculi 128
humanism 54, 55, 62, 131, *see also* secular humanism
'humanisms' 63, 85, 98, 129, 131
'humanism 1' (H1) 23-4, 28, 48, 52, 66, 98, 129, 131
'humanism 2' (H2) 23-4, 28, 48, 52, 66, 98, 129, 131
'humanism 3' (H3) 23-4, 28, 51, 98, 131, 138-9
'humanism 4' (H4) 24, 28, 51, 98, 129, 131, 138-9
'humanism 5' (H5) 24, 28, 98, 129
humanistic approaches 7
humanistic metaphors 45
human/pre-human (Gattegno) 110, 119, 120, 123, 128, 131
Humanists 22-3
hypermnesia 134
hypotheses 9, 52
'hypothesis', overuse of the term 50

'I' (Curran) 79
icons 51
ignorance (Gattegno) 115
imagist 36-7, 51, 56
I-myself 79, 85, 131
I-myself-other 82
imposing (Gattegno) 122
incarnation (Curran) 74, 76-7, 78-9, 81, 88, 95, 131
    advantages of 76
    as personal unity 78
    as submission to outer reality 81
    as the forgoing of power 80
    of the knower 91
    of the teacher 92
independence (Gattegno) 105, 121, 129
indirect derogatory intimation 57
infantilisation 134

initiative 75
inner resources 104, *see also* criteria
intellectually important ends (Popper) 11
intelligence (Gattegno) 109, 114, 118
interfering (Gattegno) 122
internal consistency 9, 11, 13, 20, 50
intimidation of readers 57
intuition 8, 67-8, 117, 119, 130, 138
investment as a prerequisite for learning (Curran) 81
irrational, role of the 67, 124

Jakobovits, L. A. and B. Gordon 26, 38

Kattsoff, L. O. 23
knowing more and more as the aim of science 9
knowledge, demonstrable vs. conjectura 1 8
Krashen, S. D. 48, 50-1, 54, 59
Krashen, S. D. and T. D. Terrell 48, 60
Kurtz, P. 22-3, 129
Küng, H. 22

labels, four kinds of 37
'Language Acquisition Device' 43, 44, 48
language and life 134
language of power 59
Larsen-Freeman, D. 71
Larson, D. N. and W. A. Smalley 90
'laying their lives on the line' (synecdoche) 64
learning (Gattegno) 116, 123
learning and acquisition 54, 133
learning as a source of stress 64
level (metaphor) 40
Lewis, C. S. 88
life experience 10-11
life in general 94
linear order (implication of certain metaphors) 44
litotes 56
live metaphors 36
Locke, J. 39
Lott, A. J., B. E. Lott, and M. L. Walsh 46
love 121
Loveday, L. 138
Lozanov, G. 60, 142

Maley, A. 7, 13, 62, 64, 77, 95, 98, 130

Man   110, 119, 120
Maples, R.   27
masculine qualities in Silent Way   129
mathematics   64
maxims   12, 13, 19, 20, 97
McNeill, A.   69, 129
Medgyes, P.   26
memorization   135
mental discipline   132
mental images   76
metaphors   35, 36, 45-7, 55, 57, 78, 95
    mixed   38, 39
method of science (Popper)   9
Micromomentary expression (MME)   52-3, 54
miracle, mystery, and authority   68, 130
'Monitor'   51, 133
More, Thomas   14
Morris, C. D., J. D. Bransford, and J. J. Franks   47
Morton, F. R.   141
Moskowitz, G.   24-5, 31, 67
music, its relation to emotions   15
mutual exclusion (implication of metaphors)   42, 44
'myself' and 'I'   25, 79
myth   8, 13, 96-7, 126

Natural Approach   133, 135, 136, 140
New Age   119, 120, 128-9
non-rational bases for action   14-15, 17

objective truth, growth of is highest value (Popper)   9-10
ogdens (Gattegno)   117, 118
Oller, J.   77, 78, 87, 93, 98
Oller, J. and P. Richard-Amato   77
ontology (Gattegno)   111, 130
'organizer' (metaphor)   48

parallel distributed processing   51
passive voice, use of the   59
past, being lived by the (Gattegno)   119, 131
patience (Gattegno)   109
PEB metaphors, *see* permeability
perceptions (Popper) 8; (Gattegno)   109
Perecman, E.   40, 46
permeability (metaphor)   50-2
    dangers in   50, 53

persistence (Gattegno)   109
physical practice   133
'pluviosity'   12
Popper, K.   7-20, 35, 50, 52, 54, 55, 67-9, 96, 107, 116, 127, 139, 144
    limitations of Popper's position   12-13
power, language of   59
pre-existing resources of learners (Gattegno)   104
pre-humans/humans (Gattegno)   107, 110, 119, 123
private resources of learners (Gattegno)   104
problems   8, 9, 11-12
psyche (Gattegno)   112, 113, 122, 128

quantum   110, 128

Rardin, J. P.   87
rational action   10
    bases for   13
rational attitude   12-13
rationalism   137, 140
Rationalists   141
realms, the four (Gattegno)   108, 111-12
redemption   76-7, 81, 88, 131
regularity (contrasted with 'rule')   133
reincarnation (Gattegno)   110-11, 128, 131
relativism (Gattegno)   120, 128
religion   7, 11-12, 22, 24, 32-3, 58, 62, 77, 81, 85-7, 89, 98-9, 115, 130, 137, 144
religious-humanistic vision   32
reminiscence   37
reserve powers of the mind   134
residual energy (Gattegno)   111-13
resources of learners, pre-existing (Gattegno)   104
responsibility   106, 121
retention (Gattegno)   109
rhetoric   15, 33, 35, 44, 54, 55, 69
Richards, I. A.   35
Richards, J. and T. Rodgers   19, 26
Rigidity, a charge against 'humanistic' methods   63
Rivers, W.   27-8
Roberts, J. T.   26
Roberts, R. C.   83
Rogers, C. R.   12, 18, 30-1, 67
    and 'redemption'   84
    possible echoes in Curran   83
routine (Gattegno)   119
rule, two meanings of   133

Sacks, O.   17

sacrament (contrasted with 'sign' and 'symbol')   94-5

Sampson, G.   51

science, aim of (Gattegno)   9

Science of Education (Gattegno)   99, 107-30, 131

Scovel, T.   27, 60

secular humanism   85, 87, 98, 129, 137

secular humanistic vision   32

security (Curran)   75, 85, 91

self and energy (Gattegno)   111

self-congruency   78

Sellers, Peter   88, 94

sensitivities (Gattegno)   109-10

sequence (implication of metaphors)   40, 44

signs (contrasted with 'sacrament' and 'symbol')   94-5

Silent Way   7, 63, 65, 101, 104, 106-7, 126, 140, 142

    EWS summary of   127

    masculine qualities in   129

simile   36

slip-of-the-tongue   38

soma (Gattegno)   110, 112, 113

spiral, downward   88

    reversal of   93

stages in Counseling-Learning   76-7, 91, 94

stance of despair   31

'standing' as well as 'understanding' (Curran)   84

Stevick, E. W.   7, 36, 45, 46, 51, 53, 56, 68, 71, 130

subordinating teaching to learning (Gattegno)   106

Suggestopedia   7, 46, 63, 65, 134, 135, 136, 143

syllogisms   59-60, 62

symbol (contrasted with 'sign' and 'sacrament')   94

synecdoche   64, 78

teacher, **god**-like position of   89

teleology (Gattegno)   111, 130

tenor (of metaphor)   35, 39, 48

Terrell, T. D.   26

testability of conjectures   9

theories   8, 9

therapeutic activity, teaching as a   66

tip-of-the-tongue   38

Total Physical Response   7, 46, 133, 135, 136

tradition (Gattegno)   110, 131, 138

Tranel, D.   87, 91

Transactional Analysis   67

truth (Popper)   10-11

Underhill, N.   21, 23
uniquely human attributes   131-2
unity, a meaning of 'incarnation'   78
unusual words, use of   59
Utopia/Utopian   14, 16, 23, 29-30, 33, 129

value of the growth of objective truth   9
values and Popper's position   16-17
vehicle (of metaphor)   35
verification in Popper's system   10
vulnerability (Gattegno) 109; (Curran)   92

Walters, J. and Y. Wolf   37
Widdowson, H. G.   128, 134
will (Gattegno)   114, 115, 128
Wilson, V. and B. Wattenmaker   31
'world 1' (Popper)   8
'world 2' (Popper)   8, 116
'world 3' (Popper)   8
'world 3' in broader sense (Popper)   12
'world 3' objects, artistic or intellectual (Popper)   9
'world 3' objects (Popper)   35, 54, 62, 96, 107, 127, 144